STUDIA PHILOSOPHIAE RELIGIONIS
19

Editor: Eberhard Herrmann

Dag Hedin

Phenomenology and the Making of the World

UPPSALA 1997

Doctoral dissertation for the Degree of Doctor of Theology in the Philosophy of Religion at Uppsala University 1997

ABSTRACT

Hedin, D. 1997. Phenomenology and the Making of the World. *Studia Philosophiae Religionis* 19. 136 pp. Uppsala. ISBN 91-22-01771-2.

This study deals with the role of phenomenology in explaining the making of the world, in particular with regard to religion. It is shown that in dealing with people's responses to life, the world and what is regarded to be beyond the known world means recognizing the restrictions provided by language and knowledge. It is also shown how this creates difficulties as to the claim within religion to express what is beyond the known and not directly available by means of ordinary language.

The author focuses on ideas within the phenomenology of religion of how to cope with this tension. He clarifies the connection between the phenomenology of religion and philosophical phenomenology in this regard. He analyses ideas concerning our relationship to the surrounding world, the conditions for human existence, and in what respect we can interpret and communicate to others our understanding of ourselves and our different life worlds.

Based on these analyses it is argued that insights from philosophical phenomenology can be applied not only to the phenomenology of religion. Ideas of phenomenology on how to gain self-understanding as well as an understanding of other people and of the world through communication and dialogue, are shown to be relevant also concerning most analyses performed within the wider field of Religious Studies.

Keywords: experience, lived experience, phenomenon, phenomenology, consciousness, intentionality, intersubjectivity, world, ego, being, self-understanding, existence, life-world, view of life, dialogue, epochē, empathy, Dasein, hermeneutics, realism, anti-realism, E. Husserl, M. Heidegger, G. van der Leeuw, W. Dilthey, R. Rorty, H. Putnam.

Dag Hedin, Department of Theology, Uppsala University, P.O. Box 1604, SE-751 46 Uppsala, Sweden

ISBN 91-22-01771-2
Typesetting: Editorial Office, Uppsala University
Printed in Sweden by Gotab, Stockholm 1997
Distributor: Almqvist, & Wiksell International, P.O. Box 7634, SE-103 94 Stockholm

Contents

Acknowledgements

Having arrived at the goal of many years of study—the writing of my doctoral dissertation—I realize that there are many friends, colleagues, and researchers worth mentioning with special thanks.

Some of the first to encourage me to go on studying with the aim of a doctoral dissertation were Dr. Kaarina Drynjeva and Prof. Jan Bergman, History of Religions at the Department of Theology, Uppsala University. The studies made me discover the philosophical aspects of the phenomenology of religion. At this time, I got into contact with Prof. Eberhard Herrmann, who became my tutor and supervisor of the dissertation now in front of you. His critical comments, his frequent and critical readings of my manuscript, and his insistent questions have been matters of utmost importance for my way of handling the material and the issues. Also, our many years' of collaboration has led to a deep friendship, the appreciation of which is difficult to express in words.

Many have contributed to my questions as to the philosophy of religion, phenomenology, and the phenomenologist of religion, Gerardus van der Leeuw. I would particularly like to mention those who have taken the time to listen, to read, and to comment and who have generously shared their knowledge with me; Prof. Jacques Waardenburg at the University of Lausanne and Geneva, Prof. John Hick, Birmingham, Dr. Jørgen S. Nielsen, Birmingham, Prof. John B. Carman, Harvard, Dr. Vitor Westhelle, LSTC, Chicago, Prof. John Millbank and Dr. Graham Ward, Cambridge.

I am grateful to the reviewers of my English, B.A. Evah Ignestam and Rev. Sr. Gerd Swensson. Some of my colleagues at the Church of Sweden Research Department have, in various ways, been engaged in my work; therefore, many thanks to Prof. Sven-Erik Brodd, Prof. Lars Hartman, Prof. Ingmar Brohed, Dr. Lennart Tegborg, Dr. Gert Nilsson, Dr. Kajsa Ahlstrand, and Dr. Jørgen Straarup. On different occasions, my friends at the doctoral seminars of the history of religions and the philosophy of religion at Uppsala University have wrestled with my texts and worded fruitful questions on my material. I have had a large amount of conversations with my friend Dr. Martin Holmberg, who, at the reading of my manuscript, has continuously brought forward constructive comments of a methodological nature.

I send all of you a very special thought—those mentioned by name as well as those not mentioned, but who have all the same meant a lot to me.

CHAPTER 1

Introduction

The Problem

Why are there so many divergent opinions regarding the failure and the success of phenomenology? To be able to answer this question we need to qualify what exactly is meant by 'phenomenology'.

Our central question concerns the role of phenomenology in explaining the making of the world, especially with regard to Religious Studies. The analyses will point at a wider application of phenomenology than the phenomenology of religion. The contribution from phenomenology to ideas on communication in terms of dialogue and intersubjectivity will be a central concern, as well. Therefore, focus will be set first on Edmund Husserl's phenomenology. We will discuss how he envisaged the phenomenon and the phenomenological method, and his proposals concerning how we ought to relate to the surrounding world, ourselves and others in accordance with his phenomenology, and why we ought to do it in this way. An analysis of Martin Heidegger's philosophy in terms of phenomenology will follow the discussion on Husserl. Focus will be set on Heidegger's ideas about the conditions for human existence, i.e., the Dasein, and how the Dasein analysis can bring forward common conditions for human life in terms of existential phenomena. This analysis points out the foundation of existence, i.e., 'being'. We will also discuss Heidegger's development of a hermeneutic of life and the role that history can play in the formation of self-understanding. His ideas about our relation to other people will also be important in the analysis.

After this we will take into consideration the phenomenology of religion proposed by Gerardus van der Leeuw. I have chosen him due to his efforts to combine philosophical and psychological phenomenology with the History of Religions for the purpose of constructing an instrument that would provide the scholar with an insight into religion as a phenomenon deeper and broader than mere historical accounts. His emphasis of an approach free from prejudice together with his proposed phenomenology brought forward a development of this particular field of religious studies. In the analysis focus will be set on the kind and degree of, and possible reasons for, the philosophical influence in his writings. This analysis will bring us forward toward the discussion of an alternative role for phenomenology within Religious Studies.

The analyses of phenomenology, and in particular the aspects of communication in terms of religious dialogue, will bring forward a discussion on realism and anti-realism in relation to ontology and epistemology, and how these positions intertwine within phenomenology. Questions on these matters will be discussed both in relation to Husserl, Heidegger and van der Leeuw, as well as in relation to the more recent debate raised by Hilary Putnam and Richard Rorty. As a result of these analyses, there will follow a proposal for an alternative role for phenomenology besides its application as the phenomenology of religion. Based on some of its central methodological concerns in terms of freedom from prejudice—i.e., 'presuppositionlessness', the suspension of value judgements and questions of thruth, i.e., 'epochē', empathy, intersubjectivity and communication—phenomenology can be applied to most disciplines within Religious Studies. In this sense phenomenology contributes to an analysis into the conditions for our relations to other people, cultural and religious traditions, systems of thoughts, etc., as well as to the communication between these.

Throughout the analysis questions of a normative nature will be brought up from a principle perspective. This is the case because the questions concerning our relationship to the phenomenon of religion is at matter. Undoubtedly there are religions, and they play an important normative role in the life of human beings.

Phenomenology and the empirical sciences both focus on human experience although there is a difference. The difference concerns the evaluation of human experience as claims to truth, how belief based on such claims can be justified and to what extent an experience may be considered as a statement of facts. Phenomenology does not deny experiences as the ground for justification and verification, but phenomenology does not exclusively relate the question of justified beliefs and true statements about states of affairs to observations. The phenomenological notion of experience thus seems to transcend the empirical and takes into consideration aspects that are not of a direct empirical, that is observational, origin.

Religions also deal with non-observational factors, i.e., aspects at the very heart of religion. Religious studies have to take this into consideration. If phenomenology in general includes consideration of non-observational factors in establishing criteria of justification of belief or verification of statements about states of affairs, this may provide a connection between phenomenology and religious studies. This thesis will first discuss the relation between philosophical phenomenology, as represented by the phenomenology of Edmund Husserl and Martin Heidegger, and the phenomenology of religion formulated by Gerardus van der Leeuw. Then, I will consider the role of phenomenology within Religious Studies, namely in what respect insights from philosophical phenomenology can be applied to other fields of research on religion besides that of the phenomenology of religion. Here the phenomenological ideas about understanding through dialogue will play a crucial role. The insights of phenomenology on how we gain selfunderstanding as well as an understanding of other people and of the world, are relevant to all the analyses performed within the field of Religious Studies insofar as they open up alternative ways of approaching a particular question or cluster of interrelated subjects of research.

Some questions have to be raised concerning both the meaning and the purpose of 'phenomenology' as applied to philosophy as well as when applied to Religious Studies. I will try to identify and analyse the various individuals of phenomenology considered as a complete system of thought, and I will also consider their mutual internal relationship. In so doing, I will focus on the following concepts and their attendant questions.

Experience: what is an experience; what constitutes an experience; what is given in experience; what does experience contribute to the content of our consciousness; what is the relation between awareness and knowledge?

Phenomena: what are they said to be; do they exist, that is, are they something real; how are they constituted?

Units and parts: what do they consist of, how are they constituted; are there any differences between the ideas of units and parts and theories of universals and particulars; are there any common features between the ideas of units and parts in philosophical phenomenology and the ideas of typologies, ideal types and types in the phenomenology of religion?

World: what is the world; how do we get access to the world; does the world exist on its own, that is, independently of us; do we create the world; what is the relation between my understanding of the world and that of other people?

Intersubjectivity: how is common understanding established; who is 'the other'; are different types of phenomenologies in agreement about intersubjectivity? If not, where do they depart from each other?

Phenomenology: is it an attempt to overcome a formal division between realism and anti-realism by oscillating between ontological realism and epistemological anti-realism which seem to be present both in Husserl's and Heidegger's as well as in van der Leeuw's writings; in what sense does phenomenology relate to the philosophical debate brought to our attention by, among others, Richard Rorty and Hilary Putnam?

The Background

Many years ago when I began my studies of the Phenomenology of Religion, my attention was drawn to the short postscript "Epilegomena" in the Dutch theologian Gerardus van der Leeuw's magnum opus *Religion in Essence and Manifestation*. When I and my fellow students were introduced to the phenomenology of religion, much of the time was spent on conveying a feeling for the atmosphere around a particular religious act, be it prayer in general or a rite of some particular type. These objects of our studies were called religious phenomena. The method in use was very congenial but it was never really clear to me what it consisted of. Was it just a sympathetic way of becoming familiar with other people's conceptions of the world? Or was it, as some of our books seemed to suggest, a genuine attempt to enter into the religious reality of another person?

I thus found myself confronted with two different applications of the phenomenological attitude which I had been taught; one with a more limited aim than the other. A certain respect for other religions was conveyed by the congenial attitude described above, which helped us feel at home with the views of life had by others. This feeling promoted both an understanding and a respect for religious interpretations and traditions other than our own. I would characterize this type of phenomenology as descriptive. Because of a recognition of shared ideas the end result could be tolerance. The main aim of this kind of phenomenology could be said to be the gaining of knowledge of how different religions and traditions approach the world.

The other attitude is, I would say, much more demanding and complex. Not only does it address the emotions but also the questions of being. Familiarity by recognition is not enough. You are also supposed to assume the role of the other, to enter their world and make it your own. This surpasses the first attitude in some aspects: it requires identification which in turn promotes renewed self-understanding through the understanding of the other mirroring myself.

These attitudes correspond to two general approaches, or phenomenologies. The first is defined as 'typological phenomenology', and the second as 'hermeneutical phenomenology'. Gerardus van der Leeuw is recognized as being the founder of the latter. He elaborates his phenomenology of religion above all in the "Epilegomena" in relation to the various phenomenologies that influenced the continental philosophy and psychology of his days.

To be able to follow his thinking I began to approach his acknowledged sources of inspiration; particularly Martin Heidegger, Karl Jaspers, Eduard Spranger and Wilhelm Dilthey, most of whom in turn refer to Edmund Husserl, the founder of modern phenomenology.

Qualification of the Problem

Let us start with the question whether there is a relation between philosophical phenomenology and the phenomenology of religion. In this book I will argue that there are two reasons for seeking an answer to that. Obviously, there are common notions and methodological labels, but are they used in the same sense? This problem has been widely discussed. The conceptual blur within the phenomenological movement has sometimes given it a bad name. I will try to show how parts of the terminology in van der Leeuw's phenomenology of religion can be clarified by tracing its origin back to Husserl. In particular I am thinking of notions like the phenomenon, epochē, eidetic vision/ideation, essence, empathy, connection, intersubjectivity, and the world. The influence from Heidegger is particularly related to the last two notions. There is also a clear influence on van der Leuuw from Heidegger's hermeneutics. This is not a sensational discovery. Everybody looking into the matter knows about this. In this thesis I want to show the interdependence in van der Leeuw's phenomenology between Husserlian phenomenology and Heideggerian hermeneutics. Ideas from psychological phenomenology, that is ideas from Eduard Spranger and Karl Jaspers, can also be recognized in this combination. This is the case when van der Leeuw deals with the problem of self-understanding and the formation of a world-view.

As far as Husserl is concerned, I want to clarify in what respect we can talk about some kind of dependence on Husserl's phenomenology in van der Leeuw's own idea of what phenomenology is. This is a much debated issue, particularly among phenomenologists of religion who discuss the question whether the phenomenology of religion can be regarded as a science in its own right independent of philosophical phenomenology. It is commonly accepted that there is a limited terminological import from Husserl; for instance, the notion of epochē, empathy and eidetic vision. By some scholars this influence is limited to the terminology without any further theoretical implications. This position is held by J.R. Plantinga, H. Spiegelberg, J.B. Carman and to some degree J. Waardenburg. Others, like C.J. Bleeker, E. Sharpe, T. Ryba, I. Sœlid Gilhus and G.A. James, are more outspoken on the influence from Husserl. Bleeker even goes as far as saying that van der Leeuw's phenomenology cannot be understood unless the closeness to Husserl is considered. It seems strange to me that no corresponding ambiguity on the role of Husserl can be found in the influence from Heidegger. One simple answer could be that van der Leeuw is explicit in his references to Heidegger but hardly mentions Husserl at all. The reason may be that van der Leeuw distances his own phenomenology from that of Husserl already in *Phänomenologie der Religion* (1925) by claiming that his own understanding does not carry the epistemological implications of that of Husserl. Instead of regarding his phenomenology as one having epistemological implications, van der Leeuw held his phenomenology to be of a psychological nature, similar to the proposals regarding the methods of approach given by Karl Jaspers and Joachim Wach.

Part One

For guidance on these analyses I have followed the central phenomenological question: what is a phenomenon? In the phenomenology of religion, a phenomenon seems to be something particular. We read about them as prayers, sacrifices and all other imaginable religious acts. In Husserl's writings it is, however, very hard to grasp what a phenomenon actually is. It is described as appearance in some sense: that which shows itself. Phenomena have to do with experience. Without experience there would be no phenomena. It is necessary to find out how Husserl conceived of phenomenon in order to see whether there is any difference between his idea and van der Leeuw's understanding of a religious phenomenon. I think this is important because it can tell us in what respect Husserl's and van der Leeuw's ideas of the phenomenon depart from each other. Is it for instance the case that a phenomenon can be wholly reconstructed and grasped in its original appearance through the phenomenological method? Or, is it rather the case that what is being reconstructed is an image of an appearance (the phenomenon in its original sense)? If the former would be the case, we can understand why these ideas have been put forward in the hermeneutical phenomenology of religion. If the latter is the case, we can at least exclude the possibilities that the phenomenon in its original appearance could be reconstructed. In such a case we are dealing with a ready-made interpretation rather than with the experience in itself.

Husserl makes two crucial distinctions. One has to do with phenomena as appearances. That is the distinction between the appearance [Erscheinung] as such and the thing appearing [Erscheinendes]. The other one concerns the distinction between experience and the experienced. To be able fully to grasp the point we have to take both into consideration.

Both the thing appearing and what is experienced can be regarded as actual awareness [conscious content] in the sense that it can be recalled and so to speak remembered as such. This indicates the important difference between the act itself and its content. It indicates further that the object of the act and the object remaining in consciousness can in practice be identical though logically different. It is on this ground that Husserl rejects the 'verificationalism' of empiricism, which builds on sense-perception. For Husserl the experienced cannot prove the experience since we can never wholly perceive an object in one single act of experience. This means that the phenomenon itself appearing in consciousness may not be totally identical with the phenomenon as appearance. There are two reasons for this. Firstly, because it is not appearance as such which remains in our consciousness but our image of the appearance. Secondly, we may require several experiences in order to fully grasp the phenomenon as appearance.

Is it possible to reconstruct a phenomenon completely? Reconstruction of the phenomena seems to be the very idea of phenomenology. This is done by putting resemblances together in units. Husserl called this 'collective associations' and he worked out a method which he called 'ideation', which means free imaginative variation. Before elaborating on that, we have to take into consideration that Husserl talks about two different types of relations, both prior to collective association. One is a primary relation, namely the relation between the parts being the constituents of a specific whole. The point is that we do not need to know how the parts relate to each other, only that they are all constituent parts of a specific entity. For example, when I was young I enjoyed building model aeroplanes. They came in paper boxes and the cover showed an illustration of the supposed outcome of my effort (I never succeeded). The primary relation was made evident by my pouring out the contents of the box on the table and looking at the large number of pieces (the parts) while keeping the illustration on the cover in mind. This kind of unity did not presuppose my knowing how exactly the parts were supposed to fit together. All I knew was that they all belonged to the whole.

The other relation Husserl talks about is relations between parts in the mind, i.e., the mental relation. It is so called, because the units it describes require some mental activity. Let us again use the model aeroplane to illustrate it. The activity of putting together the pieces of the model in the right order and in the right places corresponds to the mental relation I had imagined. The making of another mental relation would perhaps have led to an innovation of some sort.

These two types of relations constitute the collective association which for its establishment, according to Husserl, requires the method of free imaginative variation through which we will be able to distinguish the essential parts of a specific whole. As a first step, there are the primary relations which unite experiences of similar kinds. As a second step, mental relations are established by intuitive picking and structuring of the parts of a given whole. The free imaginative variation is performed by means of the mental relations, and the unity gained is a collective association based on 'family resemblance' (to use a Wittgensteinian term). The association is in other words built on a community of features that enables us to regard objects as similar or as belonging to a specific structure. Thus we can talk about doors in a general way, without paying much attention to individual differences. We know, for example, what a door is, we know where we expect to find doors and we know what to expect from them.

I have brought Husserl's idea about units and parts to attention for the purpose of putting the background in philosophical phenomenology to the use and understanding of typologies that we find in the phenomenology of religion. Let us imagine that a typology is made up where the whole is represented by prayers. Now we may run the risk of seeing the typology in terms of a primary relation. That is the case when we do not observe the variations strictly enough, i.e., the differing contents and endings of particular prayers. An observable resemblance of external appearance does not necessarily imply a resemblance of content. To avoid such a mistake we have to pay attention to, for instance, the differences in cultures and languages. So if in the phenomenology of religion we want to make collective associations, we also have to take mental relations into consideration because in them thoughts and ideas are embedded which do not necessarily become available through the primary relations, i.e., relations only between parts constituent of a specific whole where we do not need to know how these parts relate to each other.

In van der Leeuw's phenomenology, the attendant question of what the phenomenology of religion is actually about becomes acute. Is it about phenomena as such or about that which individuals say they have experienced? How can experience be communicated? What does Husserl say about this?

In order to analyse what Husserl says about this, we must pay attention, according to him, to the fact that communication of experience relates to his ideas of world-view (Lebenswelt), intersubjectivity and empathy. The two notions central to the discussion are: transcendental ego and empirical ego. We have these two different notions since the ego can be regarded as having two functions distinct from each other. The empirical ego is the Ego that acts. The transcendental ego is the Ego that reflects on itself as an empirical ego. The transcendental ego can thus be regarded as the Ego-capacity that says 'I', as in the phrase: "I fell in love".

This distinction turns out to be a problem for Husserl when it comes to communicating experiences; more precisely, the contents of what is experienced. The transcendental ego is not an entity accessible to anyone. It is instead the presupposition of self-awareness. However, we need to communicate our impressions for the simple reason that we need to share our views of life, and we need to learn from each other, thus to be able to exchange perspectives. This is important because the content of our singular experiences, i.e., the experienced, cannot be the only evidence of what is claimed by experience. Now, what we have access to is the other person's actions and sayings, i.e., their empirical ego. It is on the ground of this observation that Husserl develops his idea of intersubjectivity around the empirical ego and, not as one might expect, around the transcendental ego which logically is the prior one.

Husserl introduces his notion of empathy in order to bring two ego-functions together. We must not forget that we all have the capacity to say 'I'. Therefore we may not regard another human being only as a 'thing' (since I do not regard

15

myself as a 'thing')—not even if our access to them is no different from our access to external events. The access we do have to other people is restricted to the actions and results of their empirical egos. Both Heidegger and van der Leeuw, on the other hand, differ from Husserl on this point. They both share the view that the actual conditions of our lives are such that we transcend the mere actions and physical appearances of other people to their very being. This is possible, they claim, because 'being' as the foundation of existence, is something which we all share regardless of differences in life's contexts.

This idea provides the foundation for the phenomenological expression of the 'temporality of life' which is one of the most important topics in van der Leeuw's phenomenology. What is meant by this is explained in terms of our everyday experiences. Our ability to understand another person's experiences depends first of all on the fact that there are basic conditions of human life which we all share. Heidegger identifies these as the 'existentials', like love, care, hatred, guilt, death, awe. According to, for example, Westphal's existential phenomenology of religion, this presupposition becomes the ground for the view that religions are constructed around our experiences of these basic conditions of life. Phenomenologists use the term 'historicity' in order to talk about the temporality of life, and the expressions of the existentials through various experiences.

van der Leeuw points out that every experience takes place at a specific moment, 'now'. In this respect an experience can only be understood as a past event even in terms of its duration. We are then left with the experienced, i.e., memories of the experience. To be able to recapture the experience we have to reconstruct it. According to van der Leeuw this is something that we can all do and this ability also provides the opportunity of reconstructing other people's experiences.

The question is how far we can go in this respect. van der Leeuw seems to be of the opinion that we can transform the experience of another person into our own by empathy (he uses the term 'interpolation' [Einführung]). In that way we will understand both the other person and ourselves. Understanding experiences requires a special kind of interpretation. It is not, as we have seen above, the experiences as such which are accessible, because they are lost as soon as they have taken place. We are rather dealing with the expressions of experiences, and the interpretative technique is called the 'hermeneutics of life' which Heidegger developed, influenced by Wilhelm Dilthey. However, Heidegger himself did not introduce the idea of historicity, i.e., the aspect of history by which we can mirror our life-situations against those of others, in order to gain access to other people's lives. Heidegger developed this idea during the period of his research into time and history when he made the important distinction between 'Historie' (history in terms of a scholarly discipline) and 'Geschichtlichkeit' (history seen as an existential challenge—historicity). History, in the latter aspect, gives us an opportunity to observe how others have met the challenges of everyday life and how they have made their choices. By this we can in our turn be guided in our own choices of what directions to take in life.

To be able to analyse the links between Heidegger and van der Leeuw, I will discuss some of the basic characteristics of Heidegger's phenomenology.

Heidegger's philosophy is very complex and many of the various thoughts therein are intertwined. I will focus mainly on what Heidegger says about temporality, historicity, hermeneutics, and Dasein's dwelling in the world. The term 'Dasein' will be explained later.

By asking the following questions I hope to show the similarities as well as differences between Husserl and Heidegger: (1) Do Husserl and Heidegger conceive of phenomenology in the same way? If not, in what respect do they differ? (2) How are we to understand Dasein's temporality and what is the relation between that and Dasein's historicity? (3) How do we conceive of the world? (4) In what sense does Heidegger talk of intersubjectivity and what is our relation to other individuals? (5) What are phenomena, according to Heidegger?

There are clear differences between Husserl's and Heidegger's phenomenologies. Husserl's phenomenology is more concerned with epistemology than with ontology. Heidegger does the opposite: he starts from the question of being [Sein] itself, and seems to take it for granted that being is something which cannot be made an epistemic object, because it cannot be known. It can only be observed when it becomes clear to us in various ways.

There are similarities between their ideas of temporality. Husserl talks about the temporality of consciousness, using the terms 'retention', 'now' and 'protention' which, according to him, describe our human consciousness in its temporal quality. Husserl calls this the 'time-consciousness'. This explains why we can perform the ideative process of variation which in its turn opens to expectations (protention). Heidegger talks about the ecstacies of Dasein's temporality which are the past, the present, and the future. However, there are also some crucial differences, which concern Husserl's and Heidegger's ways of talking about intentionality and transcendence. For Heidegger Dasein is intentional in the sense of time transcending. Dasein's actions are always directed toward the future. In this respect Heidegger can say that Dasein is time transcending; every specific moment, 'now', involves a future, an expected outcome. In Husserl's case, intentionality is consciousness directed towards an object. For him intentionality means that we make ourselves aware of something.

van der Leeuw is dependent both on Husserl and Heidegger but he uses them in a particular way to suit his own purposes. Husserl's phenomenology can be said to focus on the individual performing it. Its basic aim is to establish certitude in the sense of undubitable knowledge. For Heidegger phenomenology is not concerned with this. Its objective is to make us understand what being can be like. Since we always exist together with other beings, i.e., both other Daseins and other things, this opens up for intersubjectivity. It is only in relation to other Daseins that we will find access to our own being.

van der Leeuw's phenomenology of religion is thus neither pure Husserlian nor pure Heideggerian but a mixture of the two. This becomes especially clear in van der Leeuw's definition of a phenomenon. He basically agrees with the common definition as 'that which shows itself' which we find both in Husserl and Heidegger. The problems arise when he continues the definition by reference to his understanding of religion. He talks about God as the Subject of religion, an active agent. To do that is in one sense not strange at all. In the world of religions it is quite natural to talk of God or of holiness as manifesting itself. Is it not obvious then, that that which shows itself as religious phenomena should thus be referred back to the divine active agent itself? Ought not these divine appearances in our world to be the subject of the phenomenology of religion?

I would say both yes and no. Let me begin with the no. van der Leeuw's phenomena are not phenomena in the Husserlian sense. The observed are the expressions of experiences, not the experiences themselves. In this way his phenomena are closer to the existential phenomena of Heidegger. But the way van der Leeuw studies them and organizes them in typologies by applying the epochē and the empathy and then comparing the findings, in a manner reminiscent of the free imaginative variation, comes closer to Husserl. Approaching these expressions through empathy, he uses the hermeneutics of Heidegger and Dilthey. Concerning the typologies, it can be seen that van der Leeuw is also elaborating some similarity with the pre-Husserlian phenomenology of Chantepie de la Saussaye.

We can distinguish between three different forms of phenomenologies used by van der Leeuw. I will first consider these three different approaches using the image of a triptych. One panel contains the definition of phenomena as expressions using some of Husserl's methodological approach. These expressions can be interpreted by using the hermeneutics of Heidegger. A second panel consists of typologies that have more in common with Chantepie de la Saussaye's phenomenology of religion than with philosophical phenomenology. The third panel is phenomenology in the Husserlian sense. Here the phenomenology of religion is concerned with the person performing it. This becomes evident when van der Leeuw describes phenomenology as the way in which the scholar applying the phenomenological method becomes aware of their own way in the world, in which we are struggling for control of our own lives and the situations we are living in. But this is a vain effort since, according to van der Leeuw, we will never be able to reach that control on our own. So the scholar will arrive at a kind of self-understanding which shows the need for salvation by divine grace, an insight given through the sharing of other people's expressions of their experiences. Only then will the scholar be able to continue the struggle which Heidegger identifies as a striving for power, i.e., for control, dominance and satisfactory explanation, and to accept contingency, i.e., to understand continuous change of our 'life-world' as a basic condition of life.

Part Two

The question is whether or not van der Leeuw in fact uses the phenomenology of religion for the purpose of discussing classical theological issues after all, i.e., something beyond experiential phenomena.

Here we must return to the notion of the world. Phenomenology seems to contain at its very centre the idea that the world is something we make ourselves. In the second part of my thesis I will focus on that which phenomenology states about how we create a life-world. Imagine that there is an opening within religious studies for an alternative role other than the one traditionally ascribed to the phenomenology of religion. This phenomenology would concentrate on how collective world-views and more individual views of life are established. Let me point to some of the cornerstones of such a revised phenomenology.

Here I will contribute to the discussion of the conditions on which things are said to exist. Particular attention must be paid to the distinction between epistemological and ontological realism and anti-realism for the following reasons. When dealing with religious interpretations of reality we are faced with statements that make claims in various ways about the existence of transcendent divine realities. To make things easy for the time being, let us call them all God. On the one hand it is said that we are able to attain knowledge about God. On the other hand it is said that God is beyond knowledge. So far there is no problem. Problems first arise when we start to demand that religious statements about reality must be subject to the same rules of justification and verification that we apply to other cases.

To advance further I will discuss ideas concerning the process of world establishment according to phenomenology. What can be said about the conditions of existence in general? Does phenomenology claim external objects to be 'mind-dependent' or 'mind-independent'? Is there more than one position?

As far as Husserl is concerned, there are arguments in favour of regarding him as an anti-realist. It is obvious that he does not concern himself with anything that is not an object of consciousness. Such objects exist in thought as 'thought-objects' irrespective of whether or not they exist in reality. In any case they do exist in consciousness and are thus 'mind-dependent'. Thus Husserl can be described both as an epistemological anti-realist and an ontological anti-realist. Since he seems not to be interested in whether things exist independently of our awareness of them, I would say that his anti-realism is of a weak form, at least with respect to ontology.

Heidegger's position is more difficult to define. He makes a distinction between 'world' and 'nature'. Nature is everything that exists independent of any mind being aware of it. World, however, is constituted as soon as any human being appears in existence and begins to articulate their knowledge of nature. Heidegger's view on 'nature' would correspond to a realist's position, while his view on 'world' would represent anti-realism. It seems that Heidegger holds a position of ontological realism in combination with epistemological anti-realism. This seems to be van der Leeuw's position also.

Does a combination of epistemological anti-realism and ontological (metaphysical) realism solve the problem of at least justifiable religious statements or does it just create confusion? Many researchers have pointed at the risk of philosophical confusion as the only outcome. Others, like Rorty and Putnam, have noted the problems and are currently trying to overcome in different ways the strict distinction between epistemological anti-realism and metaphysical realism.

I want to examine whether or not it is possible to open up the discussion on the distinction between the epistemological and the ontological aspects. My reason for doing so is rather trivial. I do not see this distinction as fruitful in a situation in which on the one hand we are tied to the scientific method of explanation, and on the other hand we are reminded that there are factors unknown to us that we get to know about one after the other. In my opinion, this is the lesson we have to learn from astro-physics or quantum mechanics. It is against this background that I want to make use of Hilary Putnam's philosophy, and more precisely of his 'internal realism'.

However, we cannot disregard the fact that different cultures have different explanatory models and systems of thought. This is something we learn very quickly when we meet people from other cultures or people of other faiths. Rorty's pragmatic ethnocentrism pays particular attention to this fact, and I will take the opportunity of making use of it in combination with Putnam's internal realism.

Thus, I will suggest a modified form of internal realism that takes cultural pluralism into account. Every culture carries within itself one or more 'descriptive schemes' defined by specific languages. These languages are epistemically of an anti-realist nature. They all have their own specific set of rules for verification and justification, but these are limited to their respective application. Following Putnam, we can here find an opening towards realism. Mind-independency is founded on the vacuum between the different descriptive schemes. Let us broaden this realism by making references also to the cultural and religious diversities. The attitude that springs from this opening will provide the ground on which we can establish fruitful dialogues. At the same time we ought to recognize our limitations. We cannot go beyond the rules of our descriptive schemes, nor our explanatory models with their respective linguistic limits. At an individual, personal level this means that nobody can learn everything. The individual will always be in need of other people for support and as discussion partners who can correct personal perspectives of the world. This is the very core of what is meant by the word 'intersubjectivity' when applied to the individual personal level. With regard to different descriptive schemes, intersubjectivity can be applied within the field of inter-disciplinary dialogue.

Part Three

Concluding my thesis, I will propose an alternative role for phenomenology within Religious Studies which, however, does not imply a suggestion that the phenomenology of religion should be erased from the map of academic approaches toward religion, especially not as a descriptive phenomenology.

I shall favour a phenomenology based on Husserl's concept of presuppositionlessness with 'epochē' (the bracketing of sets of ideas and values) as its method. This idea of bracketing must however not lead to a view of the world as a 'tabula rasa'. We must bring our own perspectives as a contribution to the dialogue. The epochē will remind us of the limits of our descriptional schemes so that we refrain from making judgements and consider our solutions as infallibly true. The exchange of perspectives between different people will help us to come to the most reasonable conclusion.

This requires hermeneutics that promotes self-understanding through our efforts to understand other people, both within our own cultural domain and in relation to cultures or patterns of thought with which we are unfamiliar. This type of hermeneutics goes back to Dilthey and Heidegger and has been further elaborated by philosophers like Paul Ricoeur and theologians like Werner Jeanrond. It is centred around the idea of dialogues where perspectives on life-views and world-views are being discussed and exchanged. If a common understanding cannot be reached, respect for different understandings will at least be promoted.

By relating phenomenology to all Religious Studies we extend the scope of phenomenology from being primarily related to the History of Religions to having a bearing on all disciplines. This broader application of phenomenology can be supported by Ninian Smart's definition of religion in terms of areas considered as the objects of various investigations around which we in the West have structured the Religious Studies. To combat isolationalism, phenomenology could promote an inter-disciplinary dialogue, which would contribute to a more complete understanding of what religions might be about. At the same time intersubjectivity at the individual level would also be strenghtened since there are always individuals who hold the different perspectives.

In this sense dialogue must take place between sciences in general, i.e., between their descriptive schemes. Such dialogue will also challenge the individual to re-consider their perspective on the world. In this way I hope to encourage greater mutual respect between people as well as self-respect in the individual.

Some Remarks on Method and Terminology

Most of the literature on phenomenology has been written in German, in most cases using a kind of 'meta-language' which often departs from ordinary use. This is particularly true of Heidegger who created a very special language suited for his purpose of renewing the philosophy of his time. Reading these texts can be rather difficult even for the native German.

In my work, which is directed toward English-speaking readers, I have been working mainly with commonly accepted translations into English. There are, however, occasions when I have gone back to the original texts, for example if I have felt that important nuances have been lost in the translation. Such instances will be explained either in the text or in footnotes.

An analysis of phenomenology involves explaining technical concepts, interrelated terminology, and complicated lines of argument. It is also the case that different phenomenologists ascribe different functions to technical concepts and methodological terms. My work consists largely of an analysis of how these phenomenologists develop their thoughts and ideas and how they develop their phenomenological language. Definitions and references will therefore be provided throughout the text.

Even so, there are some words and notions which I would like to draw attention to even at this stage. First the word 'experience'. In phenomenology two German words are used for 'experience', namely 'Erfahrung' and 'Erlebnis'. An 'experience' in the sense of 'Erfahrung' indicates that it can be thematisized and methodologically described and analyzed. An experience [Erfahrung] can be made an object for reflection. When 'experience' is used in the sense of 'Erlebnis', it has more to do with the ongoing process and the actual capacity to experience. The word 'Erlebnis' is translated as 'lived experience'. It refers to an experience actually lived through and it cannot be made fully available to analysis. In my text I have tried to keep the two aspects separate either by using the relevant German term in brackets and/or using the translation 'lived experiences' on relevant occasions.

Furthermore, in the chapter on Heidegger's phenomenology, I use the word 'Dasein' throughout because I have not found an appropriate translation. The often used suggestion 'There-being' does not include the aspect of 'Here-being' which is also implied in the term Dasein. Other Heideggerian words also appear in German for the same reason. I have also considered the translation of the Heideggerian words 'Sein' and 'Seiendes'. In a great quantity of English literature the word 'Sein' is rendered as 'Being' and 'Seiendes' as 'being'. I have not done so, but I have instead used the word 'being' without a capital B for 'Sein' in order to avoid the suggestion that 'Being' implies divinity as in the case with notions like 'Absolute Being' and 'Ultimate Being' or 'Supreme Being' for God. The word 'Seiendes' is here translated as 'entity' in order to avoid a confusion with 'being' [Sein].

I make no difference in this book between the words 'ontology' and 'metaphysics'. By 'ontological realism' and 'metaphysical realism' I mean the position which claims not only that a reality exists independent of us, but also that we can justify our claims to knowledge by making reference to this reality.

The position of 'ontological anti-realism' and 'metaphysical anti-realism' claims that nothing exists independent of us but theories, stories, and texts. Our truth claims are entirely determined inside of these.

'Epistemological realism' claims that the world consists of things and events which exist independent of us and our knowledge of them and that we can, nevertheless, turn these into objects of knowledge.

The opposite position, i.e., 'epistemological anti-realism' claims that there are no such things as evidence transcending truths in the sense of evidence transcending true statements. True statements can only be justified because they are based on evidence.

Apart from these qualifications, it is my overall ambition to explain my usage of philosophical notions, as they occur, throughout the text.

CHAPTER 2

Some Central Aspects in Edmund Husserl's Phenomenology

The Critique of Empiricism; the Notion of the Natural Attitude

According to Husserl, phenomenology is the necessary foundation without which an absolute, certain knowledge cannot be gained, and it is therefore prior to all other sciences. To clarify this point Husserl makes some distinctions between different kinds of understanding. First there is what he calls the 'naive' or 'natural' attitude, i.e., the attitude of everyday life, which takes for granted both that the external world of objects exists independent of our experience thereof, and that it is possible to gain knowledge thereof.[1] The problem is how and on what conditions these objects may be perceived and how judgements can be made on them.

According to Husserl, the natural attitude is significant for the sciences, especially for those which guarantee a verification of experience by empirical assessment. Experience is here reduced to sense perception as the verificational ground for meaningfulness or cognition.[2]

'Science' is regarded by Husserl as 'acts of thinking', united with each other in a special way. What qualifies these intertwined acts of thinking science is the fact that they are linked by "a certain objective or ideal interconnection which gives these acts a unitary objective relevance, and ... an ideal validity".[3]

This objective interconnection can be understood at two levels. First it can be considered as the *interconnection of things* to which we are intentionally directed by our ideas. It can also be seen as *interconnections of truths* in which this unity of things manifests itself objectively as being as it is.[4] Most of the time people do not distinguish between the two levels, but mix them up and regard these constructions as equal. Most people act in accordance with patterns of performance dictated by different sciences. But what if sciences are wrong in some aspects? In order to avoid this, we must separate the two levels in the process of establishing proof. The separation must be done with the aid of a special kind of knowledge, the foundational knowledge different from the knowledge of the natural sciences. This distinction springs from Husserl's understanding of truth and from his idea of the abstract, physical world of which the natural sciences give knowledge, although this knowledge can be ambiguous. The reason why this knowledge of the world is open to doubt is that our relationship to the world and our understanding are not founded on absolute certainty. Husserl means rather that the two levels, the unity of things and the unity of truths, are not clearly separated but

---

[1] Hammond, Howart, Keat, 1991, p 41.
[2] Kohák, 1978, p xi.
[3] Husserl, 1970b, vol 1, p 225.
[4] Husserl, 1970b, vol 1, p 225.

blurred, and this, he believes, is the reason for the confusion between opinions (doxa) and knowledge (episteme).[5]

All the sciences are always testing, designating and formulating truths and systems of truths in their specific ways. On the basis of this understanding of the sciences and their own specific rules and criteria of verification, Husserl regards the sciences as 'regional ontologies'.[6] As regional ontologies, the different sciences approach the area of things, states of affairs, relations, etc., according to their own specific interpretative patterns and by their own specific methods. Thus they present us with ontologies of their own which may differ due to the specific perspectives of each science. Husserl does not only recognize this basic scientific condition, but radicalizes it just by pointing at the fact that the world according to the sciences is always open to doubt. Thus, the certainty required by the sciences focusing on the world cannot also be a certainty within the sciences themselves. Husserl's phenomenological notion of truth[7] and his notion of knowledge are both defined in order to overcome this possible uncertainty accompanying scientific truth and knowledge. Thus the phenomenological science, being the necessary foundation for all knowledge, must offer apodictic evidence, absolutely certain, indisputable, a priori evidence. As David M. Levin states:

> The apodictic ground which phenomenological critique finally reaches is epistemically first, and expressed in terms of first principles, though it is last in being discovered, the outcome of radical reflection.[8]

The Notion of Intentionality

Together with notions like 'lived experience' and 'world', the notion of 'intentionality' is central to phenomenology. Later on I will point out the various understandings of this notion within different styles of phenomenology. In this chapter I will only give a brief account of Husserl's understanding and use of this notion. The reason for discussing it here is its crucial importance in Husserl's thinking.

The basic meaning of intentionality is 'directedness'. Our activities are directed toward something. Our consciousness is intentional. To Husserl it means that it is open to something or has a conscious relation to something.[9] The act as such, i.e., being open towards or in relation to, is called 'the intentio', and the something towards which the intentio is directed, 'the intentum'. The intentum can be both what Husserl calls 'transcendent' and 'immanent' objects. The former are objects that are transcendent in relation to the subject's mind, i.e., external objects. The latter are objects which are present in someone's consciousness and thus 'internal' in relation to the subject's mind. These objects do not

---

[5] See further below the paragraph treating the principle of presuppositionlessness, p 39.
[6] Kockelmans, 1994, pp 62–63.
[7] Husserl's notion of *truth* is rather complicated which has been pointed out by the German philosopher Ernst Tugendhat. In *Logical Investigations* he distinguishes no less than four different usages of *truth*. See Tugendhat, 1967, pp 91–93.
[8] Levin, 1981, p 8f.
[9] See Kockelmans, 1994, p 92.

necessarily have an external reality. Thus intentionality can mean conscious directedness towards intentional objects of either of these two different kinds.

There are some complicating aspects of intentionality in Husserl's thinking. The complications arise from the difficulties of the intentio to grasp the intentum when it is the constant features of objects of similar kinds or the invariants, the essences. To be able to grasp these, we must, according to Husserl, distinguish between the presented object and its very presentation, that is, between the intentional object, called the 'noema', and the act by which it is perceived, called the 'noetic act'.[10] If for instance we perceive a tree, the real physical tree is different from the perceived tree, i.e., its presentation in consciousness. Regardless of what may happen to the real physical tree, we will always carry an image of it, a memory-tree in our consciousness, and this is what Husserl calls the noema: the tree remembered as such. In this sense the meaning of the essence of 'tree' will be constituted in our consciousness as noematic content.[11] If I have understood Husserl rightly, the achievement of the noematic content of the 'tree' cannot be reached by only one act of perception, but it must be gained from several different acts imparting meaning. The reason for this is that according to Husserl we cannot grasp simultaneously all the different aspects of a material thing, because these can only be presented to us at a given moment. For the tree to become a fully noematic content, it requires a 'synthetic' act by which our memorized perceptions of a specific material object observed from different perspectives, are put together into a whole. The necessity of this operation must be seen against the background of Husserl's ideas about units and parts and against the method of free imaginative variation.

The Background to the Idea of Units and Parts

Many philosophers working with Husserlian phenomenology stress the fact that it is inadequate to talk about Husserl's phenomenology as representing a consistent pattern of thought. There is for instance a transition in Husserl's phenomenology from *pure phenomenology* to *transcendental phenomenology*. Another important shift is the abolishment of psychologism after his work on arithmetics. His revised position is explained in detail in the first volume of *Logische Untersuchungen* (LU I), subtitled *Prolegomena zur reinen Logik* (1900). However, the refutation of psychologism does not imply the abolition of all aspects of his earlier thinking. In my opinion there are some important ideas which can be traced back as early as to his *Philosophie der Arithmetik*, 1891, in order to grasp the full theoretical content of Husserl's later writings.

This early work is important because Husserl here begins to grapple with a problem that will recur later on in his thinking, namely the problem of classes of basic connections [Verbindungen] which he discusses later. It will occur again when he develops his ideas of units, parts and essential relations. It is also relevant

---

[10] Cf. Spiegelberg, 1984, p 93f. Pivčević, 1970, p 67f. Kockelmans, 1994, p 97f.
[11] Cf. Kockelmans, 1994, p 98f.

to the discussion on ideas of the process by which essences are recognized, i.e., of the free imaginative variation, which consists of comparing units of experiences and their constitutive parts.

In *Philosophie der Arithmetik* Husserl investigates and creates a theory of numbers, particularly of cardinal numbers, as did also his contemporary Gottlob Frege.[12] Here I only want to draw attention to that which he calls primary relations and mental relations and also to his definition of classes of basic connections made for the purpose of creating an opportunity to distinguish between two basic conditions under which connections/relations can be made manifest.[13] The first one, which he calls the primary relation, consists of what is given together with the conditions of its presentation. It means that this primary relation consists of its own essential parts as well as of factors arising from the 'perceptual horizon'.[14] The condition under which a primary relation is established does not involve any kind of intentional act on behalf of the observer. The relation is, so to speak, established by itself.

As far as I can see, the establishment of a primary relation depends on the conditions under which we perceive any physical object. It thus appears as a combination of its various integral parts, which constitute it as just one object, and of its external, physical surroundings, which constitute its space-time relations. Perceptions[15] by which we observe objects and the way they relate to their surroundings can be tentatively understood as a presentation of a primary relation. A physical object perceived as a primary relation presents this unity because of its own original links between its various elements. In *Logical Investigations* (LI II), investigation III, Husserl brings forward the notions of analytic and synthetic propositions. Analytic propositions obviously seem to have something to do with primary relations. He writes:

> It is, e.g., an analytic proposition that *the existence of this house includes that of its roof, its walls and its other parts.* For the *analytic* formula holds that the existence of a whole $W(A,B,C...)$ generally includes that of its parts $A,B,C...$.[16]

The analytic proposition says nothing about meaning or meaningfulness, but only refers to the implied existence of the physical parts of the whole unit.

[12] Both Frege and Husserl made use of the notion 'relation', but because of their different basic approaches they handled it differently (cf. Pivčevič, 1970, p 23f). Maybe it is due to these differences that they use the concepts [*Bedeutung*] and [*Sinn*] differently. Ernst Tugendhat provides us with a helpful way of understanding these differences between Frege's and Husserl's use of the concepts *Bedeutung* and *Sinn*. When Frege uses the concept *Bedeutung*, conventionally rendered as *reference*, Husserl uses the concept *Gegenstand*, that is *object*. And Frege's use of *Sinn* matches that of Husserl's *Bedeutung*. Cf. Tugendhat, 1967, p 35, 43n.

[13] This distinction relates to Brentano's distinction between physical phenomena and mental phenomena. To Brentano the *physical phenomena* relate to the external world as colour, sound, the landscape etc., while the *mental phenomena* relate to imaginations of a colour, a judgement etc. Cf. Patočka, 1992, p 32f.

[14] Husserl, 1970a, p 69.

[15] Although using the term 'perception' here I would like to clarify that Husserl in the actual context (Husserl; 1970a p 72) does not use this terminology; instead he uses the term 'Anschauung', understood as a psychological concept. What is discussed in relation to primary connections is how the physical phenomena can be seen, or observed, directly.

[16] Husserl, 1970b, vol 2, p 458.

The second class, the collective connections [kollektive Verbindungen], are characterized as mental relations. A mental relation is based on a mental act and is thus the result of an intentional act. According to Husserl it is necessary to introduce mental relations and mental acts because, in his view, primary relations cannot explain how diverse objects can be brought together, differentiated and counted.[17] With regard to the content—the objects are nevertheless the same objects—mental relations are only obtainable through the intentional act of reflection or thought, and they are not subject to any material variation, since they are essential relations.[18] The identification of objects as a unit or a constellation through reflection or by means of thought, creates the mental relation. It becomes a unit by virtue of the mental act whereby the ordinary objects are considered, not in their concretion, but simply as *something*.[19]

It is important to notice that Husserl talks about two different types of relations, namely mental relations and primary relations encountered by perception. The difference between mental relations and primary relations depends on how the unit is established. Mental relations are established simply by being constituted, while in the case of the primary relations, they are created by perception.[20] By associating objects into relations with each other and by structuring them into a group or a countable unit, a 'collective' comes into being. According to Husserl, a collective connection, which consists of units with common features, constitutes a 'universal'. This is a mental relation and it involves a synthetic mental act.[21]

Husserl seems to combine the two types of relations for the purpose of characterizing the pure phenomenological experience. When perceiving a rose, one may of course bluntly state: "It is a rose", without any further qualifications besides the observance of something factual, external, i.e., of an autonomous single state of affairs vis-à-vis the perceiver's consciousness. This is, however, not what Husserl is aiming at. He qualifies the experiential content, first by referring to the single parts that constitute the rose, then by characterizing these parts as forms, colour, etc., by reference to similar experiential contents. This constitutes what Husserl calls the 'associative origin of identification', which is a combination of a primary relation and the mental relation founded on association.

The Free Imaginative Variation

Phenomenology is to Husserl the method by which, when deployed correctly, we will be able to grasp the essences of things. These are the invariant features without which an object would not be what it is. The variation of our memory-images of similar things will provide us with an image of the 'eidos' of how that particular thing is in itself. The eidos is the ideal prototype or the essence of the thing.

[17] Pivčević, 1970, p 30.
[18] Patočka, 1992, p 33.
[19] Pivčević, 1970, p 30.
[20] Husserl, 1970a, p 72. Cf. Pivčević, 1970, p 30.
[21] Pivčević, 1970, p 28f. See also Husserl, 1970b, vol 2, p 458, on synthetic propositions and synthetic a priori laws.

Thus a tree requires certain features without which it would not be a tree. It may have been something else or just nothing at all.

To enable us to grasp these invariants, Husserl develops his idea of 'ideation'. It is the method for making us imagine the eidos. It is particularly in *Experience and Judgement* that this method, the free imaginative variation, is elaborated even though its basis is envisaged in Husserl's early works.

As far as I can see the variation is meant to work in the following way. First required are units of particular, memorized things/objects perceived on previous occasions. By means of this memory bank we can create, compare and put together other images that we recognize as referring to the same thing and we can, as we have seen, put them together in units. Here diverse, but similar, images are combined into a whole which may have variant particulars. This provides a memory bank, which is a mental relation, i.e., a relation that results from an intentional synthetic act. In the act of ideation we thus compare objects which have common features. From such comparisons we will be able to define those features which are common to all cases. Those features are the essences. If the essential features of the thing in question are combined in a unit, the result is the eidos or pure phenomenon, and this unit is manifested as a primary relation.

Husserl does not only introduce the notion of 'essence', but also the notions of 'type' and 'general essence', notions that will recur in the phenomenology of religion. It is important here to find out how Husserl defines these notions which might enable us to observe differences at least when the notion of type is used in the phenomenology of religion.

I have had some difficulties when trying to grasp Husserl's discussions on universals, particulars, concepts and types, and I will therefore begin by reporting on my understanding of his thinking in this regard.

First we need to observe the distinction between particulars, i.e., singular objects, and universals. A universal consists of what is common to at least two objects. An infinite, synthetic association, i.e., a collective connection, such as described above, can be related to a universal. This association is based on the original constitution of the general on the common essence.[22] This will have certain consequences for the identification of a new object of perception, similar to an earlier one. This community of essence can be transformed into concepts, like the concept of 'flower'. The identification of the appearance of the experienced is then based on recognition, in the sense of an "associative awakening of the type 'flower' established in the past, without an intuitive recollection of the earlier cases of comparison being necessary".[23]

Husserl does not apply the notion of universals only to empirical experiences, but expands it to include imagination as well. The fundamental difference between actual, empirical experience and experiences founded on imagination is the difference between particular actuality and possible particularity. Husserl explains this:

[22] Husserl, 1973, p 328.
[23] Husserl, 1973, p 328f.

If I imagine things, I apprehend in them as pure possibilities the concept of a [certain] thing. I can find this same concept in actual things; stated more precisely, in intended things which I posit as actualities on the basis of actual experience. In the transition from imagination to actual experience, these give themselves as particulars realizing the same universal which, in imagination, is not truly realized but only quasi-realized in the possibilities discerned.[24]

Husserl's idea of a universal can be clarified against this background. It is characteristic of a type that its content can be expanded through attributes ascribed to it and confirmed by actual experience. But a type can also be subdivided into particular types. This presents us with types which have individual attributes but the same typical form. We can therefore relate to 'dog' both in the sense of a particular of the universal, and as an individual.

The idea of a universal is open to further qualification by the use of attributes. I would therefore suggest that the idea of universals can be fruitfully understood if, for example, we regard the universal concept of 'dog' as the most exhaustively given description of the animal 'dog' without further reference to specific breeds like German shepherds, English setters etc. We may, however, still ask ourselves if the term 'setters' should be understood as particulars of the type 'dog' or not. This dilemma can be qualified through Husserl's distinction between non-essential types, which also takes into consideration the mode of living (Husserl exemplifies this with the German word 'Walfisch'), and essential types which are illustrated by the scientific notion of species.[25]

The Notions of Experience: [Erlebnis] and [Erfahrung]

One problem in phenomenology that we often face is the differentiated definition of 'experience' into two notions; 'lived experience' [Erlebnis], and 'experience' in a more general sense [Erfahrung]. From time to time we also find the expression 'primal experience' [Urerlebnis] which is yet another qualification. In some translations of Husserl's works into English the two notions are used interchangeably, which in my opinion can make it difficult for readers to understand the distinction. J. Findlay is explicit on this when, in his translator's introduction to *Logical Investigations,* he declares that he is using the two notions interchangeably, because Husserl himself does so.[26] There is, I think, nevertheless some point in clarifying the use of these two notions. Firstly, they play an important role in Husserl's ideas about the transcendental ego and the empirical ego and they occur in his talking about 'empathy', 'Lebenswelt' and 'intersubjectivity'. Secondly, the distinction occurs in van der Leeuw's phenomenology of religion and this requires clarification. I will therefore try to elucidate some of these distinctions and to give some reasons why phenomenologists find them important.

As we shall see Husserl agrees with the empiricists that all knowledge begins with experience. He thus, as has been pointed out by Erazim Kohák, stresses a

[24] Husserl, 1973, p 329.
[25] Husserl, 1973, p 334.
[26] Husserl, 1970b, vol 1, p 39.

positivistic standpoint inasmuch as he recognizes experience as the ground of all knowledge. But he does not, as the empiricists do, reduce experience to sense perception as the verificational ground for meningfulness or for truth.[27]

Let us begin by taking into consideration Husserl's own thinking on these two notions. I will then suggest an alternative way of formulating the notion 'lived experience', which will hopefully help clarifying the point behind the distinction. First of all Husserl distinguishes between the phenomenological understanding of lived experience and a more popular understanding of experience. When experience [Erfahrung] is used in the popular sense, he talks about experience in general, that is, whatever occupies our consciousness and whatever can be sensed by the subject by perception or sensation.[28] When we experience things and objects in external perception, the experience in question is called 'natural experience'.[29] This perception is different from what Husserl calls 'internal perception' by which we experience ourselves.

Husserl then relates this distinction to the one between the empirical ego and the phenomenological ego.[30] Although Husserl provides three definitions of the notion of 'ego' in his writings, he does of course not envisage a split of personalities but only makes the definitions in order to distinguish between them. The ego is one but it can function in at least two different ways. Simply put, 'the empirical ego' can be made an object for reflection or introspection. For example, when we transform external events, such as participation in a specific historic event into an object for reflection, the 'I' is also regarded as an identifiable object. This can be exemplified by the use of the 'I' in any kind of narrative, or in recollections of previous experiences and events, in which the I has taken part. In this kind of reflection the ego can be identified with 'the empirical ego'. It functions as the pole to which the outer events, objectified, are related to the popular notion of experience.[31] In this particular sense, experience by nature implies objectification.

The phenomenological notion of 'experience' relates to 'the phenomenological ego', i.e., to the experiencing consciousness[32] where the outer events are present as content matter, together with the understanding of the different acts forming the experiences. Experiences related to the phenomenological ego are in this sense qualified by their internal, intentional character, and are thus distinguished from the experiences related to the empirical ego.

The notion of 'the phenomenological ego' was further developed by Husserl from the time of *Logical Investigations* and was then substituted by the notion of 'transcendental ego', which refers to the ego reflecting on experiences involving

---

[27] Kohák, 1978, p xi.

[28] Cf. Kohák, 1978, p 156f.

[29] Kockelmans, 1994, p 82.

[30] There is no clear mention of the term 'transcendental ego' in *Logical Investigations*. It is interesting to observe how Husserl fights back Natorp's understanding of the ego as a non-object, the *pure ego*, that is the ego not possibly to be understood as an object. Husserl held this understanding at the time of the first edition of the LU but he seems to abandon it at the time of the second edition in 1913.

[31] Husserl, 1984/1, § 3, p 361f. Cf. Husserl, 1970b, vol 2, p 539f.

[32] Cf. Husserl, 1970b, vol 2, p 540f.

the empirical ego. This is supported by Husserl's statement in *Experience and Judgement*:

> ... by 'transcendental', nothing more is to be understood than the theme, ... of a reflection by the knowing subject on himself and on his cognitive life.[33]

Returning to the question of the interpretation of the notion of lived experience, Kockelmans makes the following observation: "Husserl makes a distinction between *Erlebnis* and *Erfahrung*. The former is called a highest genus. ... It encompasses all awareness a subject can have."[34]

What does this "encompasses all awareness" mean? Does it mean that a lived experience always takes place against the background of the total content of the mind? If so, can the notion of lived experience be substituted by 'life experience'? This is even more complicated when one continues to read Kockelman's work where he says: "*Erfahrung* is a more limited category; it is an *Erlebnis* concerning things that belong to the *real* world".[35] Husserl makes a distinction which we may interpret in the same way as was done concerning the transcendental ego and the empirical ego: a lived experience [Erlebnis] is an experience that involves a simultaneous self-reflection by the transcendental ego; this self-reflection is made over and against experiences [Erfahrungen] of the real world by the empirical ego, that is, of the surrounding world of things and objects. Thus it might be possible to talk in terms of active reflection, which connects the transcendental ego to lived experience, and of non-reflecting action, which connects the empirical ego to experience.

Collective Associations of Experience

Experiences are all sorts of events that occupy our consciousness. In this sense experience is understood as the content of consciousness—and is as such the object of reflection. As far as I can see, it is at this point we have the opportunity to relate the different aspects of experience to the idea of wholes/units and parts. By this I mean that the reflection or inner perception takes place against the background of a set of experiences [Erfahrungen]. Therefore it is important to find out what class of relation may adequately be referred to. As we have seen above, a distinction was made between mental relation and primary relation. Primary relations were those which the unity consists of in a non-intentional relation between the whole and its parts. Being non-intentional means that the establishment of the relation does not require an intentional or interpretative act. By comparison, the mental relations consist of units which require an intentional act on behalf of a subject in order to be constituted. The whole would not exist unless the parts were connected to each other by means of some mental activity.

I would now like to propose the following: Non-intentional primal relations are

---

[33] Husserl, 1973, p 49f.
[34] Kockelmans, 1994, p 82.
[35] Kockelmans, 1994, p 82.

to be understood in the same way as logic or mathematics, for example as a parallell to the formula 2+3=5, which does not require an empirical relation or comparison as proof. In the same way the primal relation can be considered to be an essential relation. However, the web of experiences include mental relations. In other words, experiences which are somehow familiar can be put together into imaginative units. It is by this process that the self-reflecting ego transforms experiences [Erfahrungen] into lived experiences of their own.

Experiences of External and Mental Objects

The notion of experience with the two aspects described above is central not only to Husserl, but to phenomenologists in general. Anything that appears can be accounted for in terms of experience. How, then, does Husserl approach the objects of experience? He makes an important distinction between presentations by perception—that is presentations of mind-independent existing objects—and representations or imaginative presentations—that is presentations of mind-dependent objects of awareness. This is important for a discussion of religious experiences, i.e., of objects that are perceived as holy, sacred etc., which will follow below.

It is worthwhile to recall once more Husserl's understanding of 'knowledge' in *Logical Investigations*. For Husserl all knowledge begins with, but does not arise from, experience [Erfahrung].[36] Our experiences may or may not have objects existing in reality. What is important is the manner in which they have their objects.[37]

Instead of speaking of psychic phenomena, Husserl uses the notion of intentional experiences [intentionale Erlebnisse]. Intentionality is an internal structure of lived experience, and what is intuitively known is an object of experience, i.e., the intentional object. The lived experience is an act which constitutes an intentional object. The same applies to all conscious acts, not only to ordinary acts of perception.[38] Therefore it is also true of dreams, phantasms, illusions etc.[39] What matters is how these objects are said to exist and not if they do exist, i.e., whether they exist independent of the conscious mind—that is as external objects—or whether they exist only as mind-dependent objects—that is as immediate/immanent objects. Here Husserl clearly holds a position different from Heidegger, for whom the question of being is the fundamental philosophical question. Husserl seems to advocate a position of ontological realism when talking about physical objects but this is not his main interest, as has been previously said. What matters is how objects are said to exist and in this regard Husserl expresses at least some soft version of epistemological anti-realism. This is particularly relevant to our discussion.

---

[36] Husserl, 1970b, vol 1, p 109.
[37] Kohák, 1978, p 121.
[38] Kohák, 1978, p 62f. Cf. Husserl, 1928, § 84, on the relation between the intentional subject, the I, and the directedness of consciousness towards something.
[39] Cf. Husserl, 1970b, vol 2, pp 557–560, Husserl, 1973, p 168, Levinas, 1985, pp 56–58, 69.

It is equally important to observe that Husserl concludes, when discussing object awareness, that one should not make a distinction between on the one hand merely immanent or intentional objects and transcendent, actual objects on the other hand.[40] The transcendent objects are transcendent in the sense of transcending consciousness. They are mind-independent. Awareness of an actual object is awareness of something manifesting itself to consciousness. In these cases Husserl talks in terms of 'presentations': an object is made manifest to consciousness by means of a perception-presentation. It might seem that presentation-by-perception would give the subject a perfect object-presence, but this is not always the case because there might be some perceptional defects which would cause a perfect perception of an object to fail.[41]

The other kind of object-awareness is one through imagination. Objects are then only present in consciousness. They are immediate, or immanent, in the sense of being imagined objects or only representations of objects. In the case of a representation, there is no present relation between the imagined object and the original object represented by its image.[42]

In his discussion on *Logical Investigations* where 'lived experience' is understood as 'conscious content', and where 'intentionality' concerns 'lived experience', Spiegelberg interprets the relation between an intentional act and its object as an identification of the intentional object with the correlate of the act.[43] Or, as Husserl puts it: "... *the intentional object of a presentation is the same as its actual object, and on occasion as its external object, and that it is absurd to distinguish between them*".[44]

This would mean that the intentional object of the intentional act, *I have an idea of the rose Queen Elizabeth,* is this rose presented as an 'immanent object'. The object is immanent in the sense that it is an image present in my consciousness as a re-presentation. This example also illustrates the meaning of the notion of 'intentional inexistence'.[45] As long as the intentional object, i.e., that which is experienced as a present object, exists exclusively in my mind without any extra-mental physical existence, it is an object with intentional inexistence. In this sense it is only an image.

> [That] means ... that the intention, the reference to an object so qualified, exists, but not that the object does. If the intentional object exists, the intention, the reference, does not exist alone, but the thing referred to exists also.[46]

---

[40] Husserl, 1970b, vol 2, p 595.
[41] Husserl, 1970b, vol 2, p 761.
[42] Husserl, 1970b, vol 2, p 594. On the difference between an object present in perception and in 'imaginative presentation' (representation), see Husserl, 1970b, vol 2, p 608f.
[43] Spiegelberg, 1984, p 93.
[44] Husserl, 1970b, vol 2, p 595.
[45] Cf. Husserl 1970b, vol 2, p 554, on the notion of 'intentional inexistence'.
[46] Husserl, 1970b, vol 2, p 596. Husserl does not use the terms 'representation' and 'reference' in the way as, for instance, Hilary Putnam does in *Representation and Reality* where the terms "always refer to a relation between a word (or other sort of sign, symbol or representation) and something that actually exists (i.e., not just an 'object of thought')". See Putnam, 1992, p 1, 1n. Husserl uses the term 'reference' in the sense that we can also 'refer' to something that does not actually exist.

For epistemic reasons all our images of gods are in this sense intentional experiences of objects with intentional inexistence.

The Ego and the World

In phenomenology, the notion of 'experience' is intimately connected with the notion of 'world'. For van der Leeuw there are, as we will see, some ways and possibilities open for an individual to live within and to relate to the world. He calls them 'the horizontal way' and 'the vertical way'.

A crucial aspect is how to trace universality in general and how to grasp it from singular events and experiences. van der Leeuw develops this thought by using the terms 'meaning', 'experience' and 'understanding'. His concepts of the horizontal way (a human being's possibilities to live in, control and interpret the world) and the vertical way (God's way of breaking into the world) play a central part for his understanding of religion and for elaborating his phenomenology of religion.

As we have seen, Husserl does not doubt the existence of the actual world, but finds the notion and understanding of the world questionable as presented to us by the empirical sciences. According to Husserl, the conditions given by our consciousness for reflecting on the world given in our consciousness are the important ones. Thomas Ryba is right when he says: "For Husserl, consciousness and possible consciousness exhaust the world. Whatever is not a possibility in consciousness simply cannot be thought in any sense."[47]

We have already seen that Husserl gives an account for experiences where the objects cannot be verified by means of sense-perception. There are even cases where he says that the object, i.e., the mental object, does not exist at all, for example in the case where one has an experience of a god (of Jupiter in this case). The problem with these kinds of intentional experiences is that, when analyzed descriptively, the object will not be found to be actually existing. The idea about such objects is, however, actual.[48]

Whatever content experiences contribute to our consciousness, they always give us an impression of the world. Thus there is a kind of self-made world that consists of ideas and impressions founded on experience. We must keep this in mind when we approach Husserl's conception of the world as 'life-world' [Lebenswelt]. During the last years of his life Husserl began to develop the idea of a life-world [Lebenswelt]. As far as I can see a consideration of this notion of the life-world will be fruitful for our analysis of the phenomenology of religion. The life-world is defined by Husserl as:

> ... the world in which we are always already living and which furnishes the ground for all cognitive performance and all scientific determination.[49]

For the purposes of my analysis I will focus only on the life-world in general, i.e., on the aspect of the surrounding world. Every one of us has an idea of the world,

[47] Ryba, 1991, p 169 f.
[48] Husserl, 1970b, vol 2, p 558f.

34

an idea which is being continuously developed. We constantly have to revise our understanding of the world, because the world itself is continually subject to change due to socio-economic, historical and other factors. All this is expressed by the notion of the surrounding world, and this is what forces people to change their minds.[50] Another relevant fact is that the ego itself is part of the life-world: I myself am part of my own life-world. It is my impression that Husserl uses the word 'life' in 'life-world' to indicate an ongoing act of experience in the same way as he does in the term 'lived experience', which indicates that a person is always living in, or going through, acts of experience. These acts also involve the self-reflecting ego. Regardless of changes of socio-economic, historical, political, etc. conditions, the self-constitutional ego is the common feature of all humanity.[51]

It is thus possible to identify the common ground for the life-world of the transcendental ego. This must be related to the observation made by Kohák who interprets the common ground as being ultimately founded in experience.

> Our experience is primary. It is our experience which leads us to posit reality as objective, not vice versa. [p 78] Any real world, even a possible real world, is necessarily an experiencable world, and, as such, ordered by subject experience. [p 88] Whatever is experiencable by one ego is, in principle, experiencable by any ego [p 88] ... while any real world must be experiencable, there need not be a real world to correspond to every experience. [p 88] ... it is *the experience* which is the datum; *the experienced*, ..., is a conclusion based on it and so cannot be used to explain it. [p 89] ... the natural world is real. But what we mean by calling it real is that it can be experienced. It is the *common way we experience* it ... that makes it possible for us to speak of a *common* world. [p 93f.][52]

As I interpret Husserl, he develops on this point his understanding of intersubjectivity. This is in line with Kohák's interpretation: "The foundations of intersubjective validity must, in the last instance, be founded in experience, not beyond it".[53] The problem which now arises is how Husserl explains our ability to experience another subject without reducing it to a transcendent object, and our ability to communicate experiences.

Intersubjectivity; The Notion of Empathy

Above, I discussed Husserl's distinction between the empirical ego and the transcendental ego. He interprets the transcendental ego as the self-reflecting ego, i.e., as the ego of the expressing 'I'. The empirical ego, on the other hand, may be

---

[49] Husserl, 1973, p 41. Thomas Ryba presents four different distinctions between different meanings of the notion of life-world based on Husserl's applications. (1) The surrounding world, the *Umwelt*, which is the realm of experiences related to particulars like individual sciences, historical periods, societal classes, world views etc., each of which moulds *Umwelt*. (2) The primordial world, the *Urwelt*, is the ideal world resulting from the suspension of all data not founded upon apodictic evidence. (3) The mediate world, the *Mittelwelt* (the notion is Ryba's own creation as he points out in note 10, p 172). (4) The essential world, the *Wesenswelt*. See Ryba, 1991, p 172f.

[50] On Husserl and the conditions of the life-world, see Pivčević, 1970, p 89.

[51] Cf. Kockelmans, 1994, pp 330–338, Pivčević, 1970, p 90.

[52] Kohák, 1978, pp 78–94.

[53] Kohák, 1978, p 79.

understood as the object of self-reflection. Thus, the transcendental ego is only self-reflecting.

Now, the question is: How can several transcendental egos be made the common ground of life-worlds, if they are only able to transcend the subject's empirical ego? In other words, is Husserl in some way trying to overcome the isolation of the subject, i.e., the subjectivity of the transcendental ego, in order to explain how we are able to experience other subjects? Without this capacity I cannot see how it would be possible for us to talk of the general feature of the life-world. Dalferth's notion of 'orientational knowledge' can be of help to clarify the complicated relation between the empirical ego, experiencing the life-world in terms of surrounding-world, and the transcendental ego, confirming that it is its own life-world that is being experienced.

By the term 'orientational knowledge', Dalferth refers to our ability to locate and organize ourselves within and in relation to the world.[54] Orientational knowledge requires some fundamental insights about who and what I am, i.e., what Dalferth refers to as 'rudimentary self-knowledge'. Self-knowledge is described from three different aspects, each answering to certain questions: (1) identifying self-knowledge answers to the 'who' question; (2) characterizing self-knowledge answers to the 'what, where and how' questions; and (3) existential self-knowledge answers to the question whether or not I exist.[55] When relating these insights to Husserl's notion of the life-world, the first and second aspects of self-knowledge—(1) and (2) above—would correspond to the aspect of the life-world as the surrounding world, while number (3) above is more in line with the life-world of the self-reflecting ego's being its own world.

It is crucial for Husserl to allow a subject to be able to experience another subject, not only as an object but as a fellow-experiencing subject. A problem originates from the idea of the ego-structure, in which Husserl can be said to be almost trapped. It is the self-reflecting ego that transcends and comments on the empirical ego. Thus, we can only experience our own experiences; that is, I cannot make the experiences of other people my own, because I can only transcend the empirical ego within my own ego-structure.[56] However, according to Husserl, I can experience the experiences of other people indirectly by experiencing their bodily behaviour.[57] What I can experience of other people and what others can experience of me are activities, i.e., the actions of all kinds that have been caused by experiences. What is common to all of us is first of all our capacity to experience both real and possible objects, and secondly that we experience in accordance with the same ego-structure. Therefore, even if we cannot experience other

---

[54] Dalferth, 1988, p 204.
[55] Dalferth, 1988, p 205.
[56] Kockelmans, 1994, p 279f.
[57] Husserl writes in *Ideen I*: "Originäre Erfahrung haben wir von den physischen Dingen in der 'äußeren Wahrnehmung', aber nicht mehr in der Erinnerung oder vorblickenden Erwartung; originäre Erfahrung haben wir von uns selbst und unseren Bewußtseinszuständen in der sog. inneren oder Selbstwahrnehmung, nicht aber von Anderen und von deren Erlebnissen in der 'Einfühlung'. Wir 'sehen den anderen ihre Erlebnisse an' auf Grund der Wahrnehmung ihrer leiblichen Äußerungen." Husserl, 1928, p 8. Cf. Kohák, 1978, pp 78–82 und Kockelmans, 1994, p 280.

people's experiences we have reasons to believe that our capacity to experience is not much different.

Furthermore, because of our common, surrounding world and its contents of sciences, languages, world-views etc., our individual life-worlds will always have similar structures and contents so that our contexts and self-understanding arising from within these contexts will not be all that different. Nevertheless there will always be limits to our capacity to identify ourselves with another person.[58]

The Phenomenon

Before turning to phenomenology as a method, I will discuss Husserl's notion of the phenomenon. To understand phenomena as things in themselves is seriously to misunderstand Husserl's intentions. Husserl almost avoids using the term 'phenomenon' in this sense and he defines instead the term 'phenomenon' through the notion of 'appearance' [Erscheinung]. A phenomenon is anything that can appear in our consciousness and can become an object of intention.[59]

This does not erase all our questions about the understanding of the notion of phenomenon. It is always tempting to read something more into this concept, besides the actual definition of phenomenon as appearance. This temptation is clearly indicated by the questions raised by the French philosopher Marc Richir:

> Peut-on dire qu'un phénomène 'est' [Can one say that a phenomenon 'is'] ...? Un phénomène se confond-il avec son essence ('Wesen')[Is a phenomenon the same as its essence]? ... Est-il quelque chose ou bien rien [Is it something or just nothing]? Est-il déterminé ou indéterminé [Is it determinate or indeterminante]? Existe-t-il ou n'est-il que simple apparence destinée à se dissoudre par le travail de la réflexion [Does it exist or is it simply an appearance which will dissolve during the act of reflection]? En quoi se différencie-t-il de l'illusion [How does it differ from an illusion]? En quoi faut-il distinguer entre l'apparaître du phénomène et le paraître de la pure illusion [How can we distinguish between the appearance of the phenomenon and the semblance of pure illusion]? ... Le phénomène est-il pensable *comme tel* sous l'horizon de la question de l'être, et s'il l'est, est-il susceptible d'être épuisé par elle [Is it possible to reflect upon the phenomenon in relation to the question of being, and if so, is it exhausted by this question]?[60]

The phenomenon understood as appearance, or as that which appears in our consciousness, carries within itself a whole cluster of connections. 'Phenomenon' is related to the notion of 'essence', which in its turn seems to be related to 'meaning'. Meaning then is related to truth-constituted evidence. It is a correspondence between the object of intention and its intentional correlate

---

[58] In the fifth of the Cartesian Meditations Husserl says: "In any case then, within myself, within the limits of my transcendentally reduced pure conscious life, I *experience* the world (including others)— and, according to its experiential sense, *not* as (so to speak) my *private* synthetic formation but as other than mine alone ..., as an *intersubjective* world, actually there for everyone, accessible in respect of its Objects to everyone. And yet each has his experiences, his appearances and appearance-unities, his world-phenomenon; whereas the experienced world exists in itself, over against all experiencing subjects and their world-phenomena." Husserl, 1988, p 91.

[59] Levinas, 1985, p 129, n58.

[60] Richir, 1987, p 17.

Husserl makes a distinction between the phenomenon as (1) appearance and (2) that which appears.[61] Both (1) and (2) concern the temporality of the phenomenon, and the very givenness of the phenomenon.

The appearance, taken as what Husserl calls self-givenness, is always present at a given moment, 'now'. When reflecting on the recollection of the phenomenon, (whatever it may be), it is no longer present in that primal sense. We have, in our consciousness, a memory of it. It has undergone a transformation from being a phenomenon of cognition to an object of cognition. The distinction may therefore be understood as a distinction between the phenomenon as 'phenomenon of appearance', i.e., of the appearance in a now-phase, and the phenomenon as 'appearing-object', i.e., as memory.[62]

According to Husserl we experience the world as a 'typified' world, i.e., as a multitude of types.[63] These types appear in our consciousness as phenomena. Husserl's distinction between 'phenomenon as appearance' and as 'that which appears' can now be applied in the following way. First, we have the appearance of something not yet identified. This would correspond to 'appearance'. The identification of this something—for example as a new dog—takes place by means of the associative awakening, based on recognition. This identification would then correspond to 'that which appears'. It is the phenomenon in this latter sense which constitutes the cognitive content upon which we can reflect, and which qualifies our experiences as conscious experiences. When the attention of our consciousness is directed towards both the appearance and towards something in front of us, the 'phenomenon' is identical with the 'intentional object'. In cases where there is a consistent correspondence between the intended and the given, truth is established. The experience of truth is then the same as the experience of evidence.

Before returning to Husserl's notion of phenomenon and to the conception of the possibility of definition put forward in this thesis, we must consider the method for grasping the phenomena.

The Phenomenological Reduction

Having made some basic inquiries into some notions central to Husserl's phenomenology, it is time to focus on his understanding of the phenomenological method. Let us begin with the relation between phenomenology regarded as science and other sciences.

All sciences are concerned with 'truth' or, more precisely, with truth in relation to the various issues treated under specific conditions in different contexts (see for example 'life-world' meaning 'surrounding world' above). In this sense we can say that there are different fields of science, all of which present us, respectively, with different units of truths. 'Truth' here indicates some sort of relativism. How-

[61] Husserl, 1970c, p 9.
[62] Husserl, 1970c, p 9. Cf. Jan Bengtsson's translation *Fenomenologins idé*. Daidalos. Göteborg 1989, p 51f.
[63] Husserl, 1973, p 331.

ever, Husserl's aim is to provide a scientific method free from all sorts of relativism. It is this tension that is the epistemological background for his phenomenological method. i.e., the phenomenological reduction.

The Principle of Presuppositionlessness

As we saw at the beginning of this chapter, Husserl builds his phenomenology around his criticism of empiricism. His critique took the erroneous natural attitude as its point of departure, i.e., the attitude of everyday life, in which it is taken for granted that the external world with all its varieties of objects exists, independent of our experience thereof. According to Husserl, this attitude would also grant the possibility to gain knowledge about the world.[64] The main problem concerns the question of how and under what conditions we experience objects and how we can make judgements about them. In perceiving an object we might get the idea that we are experiencing it in its fullness. This is, however, not the case.

Husserl's idea of the constitution of universals is based on the fact that we must compare and associate several observations in order to grasp the full essence of a phenomenon. We only comprehend parts of this fullness by actual perception. Failure to realize this is the cause of the basic error, which consists of a blurring of the distinction between opinion, doxa [δοξα], and knowledge, episteme [επιοτημη].[65] What is important for Husserl is providing the means by which to grasp phenomena in consciousness without any preconditions, which may determine our subsequent reflection by some previously given understanding of their identity. To be able to do this we first have to suspend all theories and beliefs about ourselves and about the world, suggested to us by the sciences. This is the central core of the idea of 'transcendental reduction'.

The principle of 'presuppositionlessness', which is much debated, should not be understood in its very strict, static, sense as indicating a total suspension of description by comparison.[66] It is closer to Husserl's way of thinking to relate the principle of presuppositionlessness to his idea of relativity and certitude. When approaching the objects of the world, we might state that a certain surface, for example a table-top, is flat when seen through the eyes. However, this is maybe not the case at all, since by using certain instruments, such as a microscope, we can observe that the table-top is in fact uneven, and that it looks more like the surface of the moon. The principle of presuppositionlessness is therefore rather to be seen as a precaution, and it is required until we know when to make statements and when to rationally raise doubts. This principle should therefore be applied within the context of the phenomenological reduction.

---

[64] Hammond, Howart, Keat, 1991, p 41.
[65] Levin, 1970, p 4. Cf. Kolakowski, 1987, p 6.
[66] Cf. Haglund, 1977, p 40f. Also Barbosa da Silva, António, 1982, p 28f.

The Epochē

In order to be able to understand Husserl's idea of the epochē it is important to discuss further principal distinctions. I will begin with his notion of transcendence and of immanence and then move on to the distinctions between (1) the real [real] and (2) the genuine [reell].

When Husserl talks about the transcending aspect of the natural attitude or natural thinking, he refers to physical things/objects in their actual existence. This is transcendence in its real sense. Transcendence in its genuine sense is the experience of these physical things.

Concerning immanence he makes the same distinction. Real immanence is exemplified as consciousness of a psychical event. Understood in its genuine aspect, immanence means consciousness as self-consciousness.[67]

At least two activities should be suspended by the means of phenomenological reduction: (a) all forms of natural thinking, i.e., all transcending conceptions—firstly because of the obvious risk of confusion between opinion and knowledge, and secondly because of the relativity of the surrounding world, with the sense of the existing multitude of sciences—all with their own truths or sets of truth. Suspension here means suspension of beliefs in real transcendence. This leads Husserl to yet another suspension: (b) the aim for real immanence, i.e., the objectification of psychical events into objects. This is a crucial point.

On the one hand it means the bracketing of the phenomenon in its sense of 'the appearing thing' [Erscheinendes], which it is possible to recapture as a memory image of the 'phenomenon as appearance' [Erscheinung]. On the other hand it seems possible to understand Husserl in such a way that this memory, or the enduring phenomenon as conscious content, can be recollected in some sense as appearance [Erscheinung].[68] This might be explained against the background of Husserl's idea of the memory as always being a constituent part of our consciousness and thus as transcending temporality in the sense of the past, the present, and the future.[69] This means that whatever we reconstruct is only present in the sense of images, as re-presentations of the original. At the same time it is important to underline that Husserl, when talking about recollection, clarifies that appearances in recollection is different from those of perception. In recollection, that which appears is presented, which means that in the act of re-presentation it is only images of the object that are placed before us, not the object itself.[70]

Reduction in the sense of (a) and (b) above does not lead directly to phenomenological insight. This can only be reached through the process of ideation or the ideative abstraction. It is by means of ideation we can grasp the general essences.[71] According to Husserl, we must move from mere examples, from singular types, to ideally posited universals. It seems fruitful to me to understand (b) above as the reduction of temporal objects, of the spatio-temporal phenomena

[67] Bengtsson, 1989, p 43, n5.
[68] Husserl, 1992 §§ 12, 15, 17, 24, 25, 27. See pp 52–83.
[69] Husserl, 1992, pp 76–79.
[70] Husserl, 1992, p 63f.
[71] Spiegelberg, 1982, p 95f.

which endures for the purpose of grasping the ideal, universal, general essence. This we can only do through an act of ideation:

> In an 'act of ideation' that we perform on an object, or rather on an experience in which we have something as an object, the existential aspect recedes into the background, and it is because the existential aspect recedes into the background that, according to Husserl, we are able to penetrate down to the 'essence'. 'Species', according to Husserl, are discovered in just such 'acts of ideation'.[72]

The Accessibility of Phenomena for Reflection

We have now reached the point where we can conclude the analysis of Husserl's notion of phenomenon, by discussing the problem of the accessibility of phenomena. I will do so by responding to some of Marc Richir's questions introduced above.

(1) Can one say that a phenomenon 'is'? The 'is', in the phrase "a phenomenon 'is'", I interpret to mean "a phenomenon exists by itself". In the discussion of intentionality it was made clear that in *Logical Investigations* Husserl made no sharp distinction between the 'intentional object' and the 'correlate of the act'. The idea was to be revised in his later works. As we interpret the phenomenon as an unidentified 'something' (to which the conscious act directs itself), the phenomenon, in its aspect of appearance, corresponds at least in some sense to the intentum, that is, to the something. The 'noema' corresponds to the [Gegenstand], i.e., the object belonging to the intentum.

The distinction between the intentum and the intentio can only be made in a logical sense. This would lead to a negative answer to question (1). We still have yet another opportunity to approach this question by taking note of the distinction between the question of intentional in-existence and intentional existence of the intentional object. Obviously, Husserl is mainly interested in the intention, in the presentation of the object in consciousness. There are two possibilities: (a) the intention, the reference to an object, exists but the object itself does not, or (b) if the intentional object exists, then the intention coexists with it. Thus, there seem to be two possibilities: in imaginations, phantasies, dreams, etc., the intentional object (here interpreted as the phenomenon) does not necessarily exist by itself, but in relation to actual experiences of perception it exists as intentional object. This also clarifies at least to some extent Husserl's notion of 'Gegenwärtigung' and the different levels of being present.

I think that this also answers Richir's questions: Est-il quelque chose ou bien rien? Est il déterminé ou indéterminé? En quoi se différencie-t-il de l'illusion? En quoi faut-il distinguer entre l'apparaître du phénomène et le paraître de la pure illusion?

(2) Is the phenomenon confused with its essence? Against the background of what has been realized I am prepared to answer question (2) positively so far, although a clarification is needed. Following Husserl's discussion and investigation of universals (general essences), and the question of temporality, it seems

---

[72] Pivčević, 1970, p 62.

possible to say that the phenomenon is a form of conscious content which in one aspect appears as the duration of essence. Although answering the question positively, I am not prepared to go as far as saying that a phenomenon consists of pure essence. The phenomenon seems instead to present us with essence in various degrees, and this follows the idea of attributing properties to a universal.[73] Further, if meaning, in the sense of evidence, is identical with essence, then essence would only be present in cases where there is an experience of corresponding consistency between what is intended and what is given. According to Husserl, that is what constitutes evidence. If this is in fact the case, it would in turn create a serious obstacle to the understanding of essence in the experience of intentional acts of intentional in-existence, because we could not in such cases say what is the given entity.

(3) Is it possible to talk about a phenomenon? Can we communicate our experience of a phenomenon? As we have seen, the central problem for Husserl was how to express ourselves with absolute certitude. In the process of reaching that position he introduced all those everyday traps, created by our object-language and by any absolute obedience to science; traps which we would fall into if we were not able to manage to avoid following the 'natural attitude', i.e., giving our consciousness a 'carte blanche', as a centre to the formulation of ideas, impressions, and knowledge. For this purpose we would have to approach ourselves and our life-world by means of 'presuppositionlessness' applied in terms of the epochē. We would distinguish between the phenomenon as appearance, and that which appears. As contents of consciousness, phenomena are stored in memory, although not in all their aspects. Brought together in consciousness they are, in one sense, always present, and we always have the mental capacity of recollecting them. This is an indication of our ability to communicate them to other people, at least as memories and impressions. At the same time it seems clear that the principle of epochē should not always be applied, since the phenomenological reduction is only observed during the perceptual act by which we establish a conscious content as knowledge. However, phenomenological reduction preceeds, but does not facilitate, ordinary communication. In order to communicate we have to return to the social, scientific, and historic context in which we actually live our daily lives.

One problem still remains, and that is what I would call the 'fragility of essences'. How can we be sure that we communicate what is essential? This is an obvious problem widely observed and it is also one of the central problems of this thesis; how can anyone from the point of view of subjectivity, conclude with certainty something that is universal if, in the end, I can never go beyond my personal ability to comprehend the essence of a phenomenon? The most fruitful way to approach this problem is observing Husserl's important distinction between the experience and the experienced. This can at least make us observant of the fact that we do not communicate experience. What we communicate is the

---

[73] I am here thinking about what may implicitly be understood as our uncapability of a complete grasping of the essence once and for all of a specific experience.

experienced. This does not mean that we are unable to communicate essences, but that we must be aware of the fact that it is not self-evident that this is the case. We might as well communicate images which is something altogether different.

Before embarking on an analysis of what Heidegger says about phenomenology, I will sum up some points from this chapter which will also appear in the following analyses.

1. As far as a phenomenon can be defined, it is 'appearance'. Husserl makes the important distinction between the phenomenon as appearance [Erscheinung] and the appearing thing [Erscheinendes]. He makes the corresponding distinction between the experience and the experienced, that is, between the act and its content.

2. The act of experiencing is the act in which the ego is actively involved. This is a lived experience [Erlebnis]. The ego involved in lived experiences is the transcendental ego. This ego is differentiated from the empirical ego, from the physical person. The transcendental ego is the self-reflecting ego, that is the 'I' in sayings like "I fell in love". When we observe other people, we can only observe them as empirical egos. The transcendental ego cannot be observed.

3. Phenomenology is first of all a method of approaching the world. It is a reductive method, and its main aim is to reduce influences and a priori understandings about the world originating from the sciences. The reduction is necessary because, according to Husserl, the world of the sciences is always open to doubt. The principle of presuppositionlessness carried out by the bracketing termed 'the epochē' is the cornerstone of the method. According to Husserl, phenomenology is first of all an epistemological concern.

4. Phenomenology aims at clarifying the 'eidos' of something. The 'eidos' can be said to be an essential unity. All the different essences of a particular object cannot be grasped by one single act of experience. According to Husserl, we must return to the object in question on several occasions.

5. To be able to gain some ideas about the type of object we are dealing with, we can compare it to objects which we already know about. This is done by the process which Husserl calls the 'free imaginative variation'. The variations take place within time-consciousness by which we can refer back to past experiences, and recollect them in terms of content, compare them with the present. Thus we can point out a future expectation. Husserl describes this by using the terms of 'retention' and 'protention'.

6. To avoid egoism and idiosyncratic ideas of the world we must relate to other people. Communication between ourselves and others should be performed with an attitude of empathy. This is so because of what was said under point (2) above. As we cannot observe the transcendental ego of another person, being the central pole in every individual consciousness, we have to relate to the empirical ego. Doing this we must avoid regarding the other person as an object or as a thing. These are some of the ideas behind Husserl's notion of intersubjectivity. The empathic attitude should be observed because of the fact that the conditions, on which we approach and observe other people, are the same for all of us, and no single one of us wants to be regarded as a thing.

In the following chapter we will see how Heidegger departs from Husserl's ideas of phenomenology. It will also be clear that it is on the points made above that we can find connections between Husserl and van der Leeuw. The same points will again be of central importance for our discussion on the role of phenomenology within Religious Studies in the final chapter. Heidegger's contribution will be of a different nature. The main difference between Husserl and Heidegger is in determining the focus of the phenomenological investigation. Husserl focuses on epistemology and Heidegger on ontology. Moreover, ontology does not mean the same for Heidegger as for Husserl.

CHAPTER 3

Heidegger on Phenomenology

The Project of Fundamental Ontology

By taking the ontological question as the point of departure for his philosophy, Heidegger clearly distances himself and his understanding of phenomenology from the thinking of Edmund Husserl.

For Heidegger, phenomenology concerns the question of 'being'. In his *The Basic Problems of Phenomenology*, based on his course of lectures during the summer semester at the University of Marburg/Lahn in 1927, Heidegger presents his idea of phenomenology in relation to the phenomenological movement of the time. In the introduction he states the following characteristics and distinctions:

> Hitherto, phenomenology has been understood, even within that discipline itself, as a science propaedeutic to philosophy, preparing the ground for the proper philosophical disciplines of logic, ethics, aesthetics, and philosophy of religion.[1]

Arguing against this understanding, he continues:

> We shall maintain that phenomenology is not just one philosophical science among others, nor is it the science preparatory to the rest of them; rather, *the expression 'phenomenology' is the name for the method of scientific philosophy in general.*[2]

What is here meant by 'scientific philosophy' can be illuminated by turning to *What is Philosophy?;* the work where Heidegger, by reference to Aristotle, defines 'science' as equivalent to the Greek word ἐπιστήμη [episteme]. 'Science' should not be understood according to a modern conception of the word; rather that philosophy as science is ἐπιστήμη θεωρετική [episteme theoretike], speculative knowledge.[3] That which is grasped in this speculative manner of philosophizing is that the "first principle and causes [that] thus constitute the Being of being".[4] In the following my reading of Heidegger's philosophy will be directed both to Dasein and its ways of being and also towards things and objects of the world, i.e., entities that are not Daseins.

As pointed out by Burt C. Hopkins, Heidegger's phenomenology is tied up with his understanding of ontology.[5] Being is the theme of his ontology: "At present we are merely asserting that being is the proper and sole theme of philos-

---

[1] Heidegger, 1982, p 3.
[2] Heidegger, 1982, p 3.
[3] Heidegger, 1989, p 55, 57.
[4] Heidegger, 1989, p 57.
[5] Hopkins, 1993, p 82.

ophy. Negatively, this means that philosophy is not *a science of* beings but of *being* or, as the Greek expression goes, *ontology.*"[6]

The distinction between vulgar and fundamental ontology which Heidegger makes is of crucial importance when trying to grasp the central role ascribed to being in his phenomenology. According to Robert Brandon, "vulgar ontology is the cataloguing of the furniture of universe [which in some cases] takes the form of a specification of *criteria of identity* and *individuation* for entities of those kinds".[7] In the following I will make clear that this mainly refers to Heidegger's notion of 'nature' while the fundamental ontology relates to his notion of 'world'. This will be further discussed below.

Fundamental ontology requires a characterization of ontological categories, and therefore it is said to go deeper than vulgar ontology, because it does not enquire into what 'is', but rather into what being itself can be said to 'be'. Heidegger recognizes first of all two ontological categories of being: the readiness-to-hand/availableness [Zuhandensein], and the presence-at-hand/occurrentness [Vorhandensein]. Availableness describes the ways of being of an entity and it is defined by means of the usage of this entity.[8] The availability of, say, a hammer is found in its usefulness for hammering. That which Heidegger calls 'equipment' are the things that are available for us due to their purposefulness.

Things and objects which are only present-at-hand/occurrent are not always available for us for different reasons. (1) Misfunction may make an object fail in usefulness.[9] The thing or object, say a broken jar, is still present-at-hand in the sense that we know what a jar is, in terms of an object, but the jar in question is not available in terms of its function. (2) Things may be present-at-hand when they are only objects for reflection on their nature and properties.[10] Such reflection gives only a theoretical knowledge which does not allow the use of the object. (3) A third sense of present-at-hand, 'pure occurrentness', in Dreyfus' terminology, is related to the breakdown of the surrounding world, such as dramatic social change, or to an individual's experiences of the world as falling apart.[11] Even if there is still a world present, the subject no longer recognizes it as available.

The Question of 'being' [Sein]

Before going any further I will present some central points relating to Heidegger's use and understanding of the notion of 'being'. There is in my opinion an obvious risk—especially for a theologian—of reading into the notion of 'being', when spelled with a capital B, some sort of divine, supreme nature. It is therefore important to note that Heidegger himself finds that:

[6] Heidegger, 1982, p 11.
[7] Brandon, 1993, p 46.
[8] Dreyfus, 1991, p 63.
[9] Dreyfus, 1991, p 70f., Dreyfus and Hall, 1993, p 6f.
[10] Dreyfus and Hall, 1993, p 7f.
[11] Fell, 1993, pp 68–72.

> The idea of being as a superior power can only be understood out of the essence of 'being' and transcendence, only in and from the full dispersal belonging to the essence of transcendence ..., and not by an interpretation referring to an absolute Other [*Du*], nor to the *bonum* [the good] as value or as the Eternal.[12]

And he concludes that this problem, which is the problem of transcendence, must be founded in an inquiry about temporality and freedom. It is only on the basis of such an inquiry that the extent of the identification of being with a superior power can be shown, or as something holy belonging to a transcendent reality proper. The first step in Heidegger's analysis is therefore an investigation of 'being' by means of analyzing the transcendence of Dasein.

An initial problem of the analysis of 'being' is that, according to Heidegger, we are not capable of grasping 'being' in its full meaning. But the moment the question is raised, some knowledge of 'being', in terms of existence, seems to be at hand. This present tense of the verb, 'is', does not imply knowledge of what it is. The use of the present tense (is) only indicates that something is present, directly or indirectly.

The crucial question is what characterizes 'entities' [Seiendes] as entities, since the 'being' of an entity is not in itself an entity.[13] However, our understanding of 'being' is initially grasped on the basis of entities. The difference between 'being' [Sein] and entities [Seiendes] is the one between the revealing and the revealed. According to Heidegger, this is a fundamental difference which must be upheld. It is also the difference between 'being' itself, (i.e., the most general quality of entities), and particular entities; or in other words, between presence and present things.[14] It is this difference between 'being' and entities which constitutes the 'ontological difference'.

In negative terms 'being' can be defined as not being an entity, nor a process nor an event. Even so it does not tell us much about Heidegger's intentions when using this notion. It does, however, indicate a possible interpretation of the notion of 'being' as the fundamental expression of something's existence. It is therefore not possible to identify 'being' as some sort of abstract object, nor as a concealed, though active, agent as a giver of existence. According to Richard Rorty, Heidegger does not answer the question of what 'being' is, because we lack a meta-vocabulary by which we can analyse it. In this sense 'being' is the first component, but not the first principle because Heidegger wants to break free from what he calls the *onto-theology*. Heidegger's reason, as Rorty suggests, might be:

> ... not that he wants to direct our attention to an unfortunately neglected topic of inquiry, but that he wants to direct our attention to the difference between inquiry and poetry, between struggling for power and accepting contingency.[15]

---

[12] Heidegger, 1984, p 165, n9. N.B. The brackets are not mine.
[13] Heidegger, 1993b, p 26. Cf. Heidegger, 1972, p 6. In the following I will translate the German term *Seiende*s with *entity* rather than being. To talk about beings [Seiendes] in relation to being [Sein] may lead to unfortunate misunderstandings.
[14] Spinosa, 1993, p 276.
[15] Rorty, 1993, p 215.

This, Rorty suggests, means that Heidegger on the one hand wants to draw attention to the difference between a scholarly investigation of what 'being' is or could be—which seems impossible to achieve fully (to struggle for power)—and the richness of poetic langugage—which can be used to express the seemingly obvious for which we lack an appropriate explanatory language (to accept contingency). An example of this could be the description of love as electro-chemical processes in the brain, triggered by hormons, and poetic expressions of love. For Heidegger, language is a key to the question of what philosophy actually is. Thus the fundamental philosophical task is centred around the question of 'being' and Heidegger points out that the question of 'being', in which Dasein reveals itself, is made possible through the direct impressive force of the most elementary words of language.[16]

Poetry, according to Heidegger, is therefore the most intimate way by which we may reach the original realm captured by the Greek word 'λόγος', which means 'co-respondence'. In relation to language in general he says:

> But because poetry, if we compare it with thinking, is in the service of language in an entirely different and distinctive way, our discussion, which follows philosophy's thinking, necessarily leads to a discussion of the relationship between thinking and poetic creation.[17]

'Being' and Metaphysics

To be able to enter into an analysis of Dasein, i.e., of human existence, it is necessary for Heidegger to isolate Dasein from other things and objects which also exist. This approach requires neutrality, which implies "... a peculiar isolation of the human being ... [which] ... is the *metaphysical isolation* of the human being".[18]

This approach leads us toward a central theme in Heidegger's phenomenology, namely the one of 'uncovering'. It is my intention to show how by the notion of uncovering we may understand the central relation between Heidegger's philosophy, i.e., ontology, and his view of metaphysics. When he approaches traditional ontology and especially metaphysics, he should not be thought of as an anti-metaphysician. His intention is rather to revitalize metaphysics by means of pointing out the original meaning. For Heidegger, metaphysics has to do with how the *ground* of 'being' [Grund] can be expressed. It is not easy to find the most appropriate translation into English for Heidegger's use of the term 'Grund'. Depending on the context, English words like 'reason', 'ground', 'cause', 'fundament', or 'basis' may be appropriate. I will try to clarify this by alternating between these various translations.

---

[16] See Heidegger, 1993c, where the original muses *Melete* (Care or Practice), *Mneme* (Memory) and *Aiode* (Song) are essential aspects of poetry. For Heidegger these aspects are the saying of 'being'. Translator's Foreword p. xii. Rorty gives us further examples of essential words: *Alétheia, Physis, Idea, Energeia, Hypokeimenon, Hyparchein, Actualitas,* Objectivity, Freedom, Will, etc. Rorty, 1993, p 209f.
[17] Heidegger, 1989, p 95.
[18] Heidegger, 1984, p 137.

48

Towards the end of *The Metaphysical Foundations of Logic* we are given that which I regard as the fundamental qualification of the term 'Grund': "... if being establishes world-entry for entities, i.e., lets entities be understood as entities, *then 'ground' belongs essentially to being.* From this ensues the true metaphysical sense of the principle of ground."[19]

The notion *world-entry* requires an explanation. Heidegger makes an important distinction between 'nature' and the 'world'. The 'world' is Dasein's conception of the external surrounding things and objects belonging to 'nature', which in its turn exists independent of Dasein:

> World is only, if, and as long as a Dasein exists. Nature can also be when no Dasein exists. ... Nature can also be without there being a world, without a Dasein existing.[20]

The notion of 'world' points to a philosophical problem of how someone can have an intentional relation to something of which that someone is themselves a part, i.e., to the world. Heidegger solves this problem by using the notion of 'transcendence'. In *The Metaphysical Foundations of Logic*, he distinguishes between two basic philosophical concepts of transcendence. The first is the epistemological transcendence, which is derived from the meaning of the term 'transcendent' in contradistinction to the 'immanent'. The immanent is what remains within the subject's consciousness. It follows that the transcendent is that which does not remain within, but outside of consciousness. Thus, Heidegger concludes that transcendence "... is taken to be the relationship that somehow or other maintains a passageway between the interior and exterior ...".[21] The problem of how such a passage is possible must be solved by an analysis of the notion of Dasein: "... the problem of transcendence depends on how one defines the subjectivity of the subject, the basic constitution of Dasein".[22]

Thus, according to Heidegger, the question becomes the one of how and "... whether the essence of subjectivity can be grasped, ..., through a rightly understood transcendence".[23] The epistemological concept of transcendence, founded in the philosophical problem of cognition, is to be distinguished from a theological concept of transcendence. In this sense transcendence is both the opposite of the contingent and beyond all contingency "... as that which conditions it, as the unconditioned, but at the same time as the really unattainable, what exceeds us ... Transcendence is stepping-over in the sense of lying beyond conditioned beings".[24]

While 'epistemological transcendence' refers to relations between subjects and objects, 'theological transcendence' is the relation between contingent entities in general (which includes subjects and all possible objects), and unconditioned being. Unconditioned being is the ultimate postulate of most religions,

---

[19] Heidegger, 1984, p 218. I have modified the translation by using the word 'entities' instead of the word 'beings'.
[20] Heidegger, 1982, p 170, 175.
[21] Heidegger, 1984, p 160f.
[22] Heidegger, 1984, p 161.
[23] Heidegger, 1984, p 161.
[24] Heidegger, 1984, p 161.

whether called 'God', the 'Absolute Supreme Being', or whatever literal meaning of the word 'transcendent' being used. The being-beyond here indicates an onto-logical difference in the degree of being, namely the difference between God the Creator and creation. No such difference is made under the epistemological concept of transcendence.[25]

Heidegger does not see a definite barrier between the two concepts of tran-scendence, but he can think of them as mutually dependent.

> ... once the epistemological conception of transcendence is granted, ... then a being is posited outside the subject, and it stands over and against the latter. Among the beings posited opposite, however, is something which towers above everything, the cause of all. It is thus both something over against (the subject) and something which transcends all conditioned beings over against (the subject). ... So, inquiry into the possible constitution of the transcendent in the epistemological sense is bound up with the inquiry into the possibility of knowing the transcendent object in the theo-logical sense.[26]

Transcendence constitutes Dasein's possibility to relate to entities. Thus Dasein is itself the passageway between its own 'being' and other entities. The gap thus bridged is not a gap between subjects and objects but between Daseins and enti-ties. According to Heidegger, entities only become manifest through the tran-scending Dasein. Thus, "Dasein can learn to relate to entities in diverse ways and to confront entities only because Dasein, as existing, is in a world, ...".[27] The world is that towards which the transcending subject, Dasein, transcends. For the Dasein to transcend then means to realize itself in a world. Heidegger describes this phenomenon of Dasein's transcendence as *being-in-the-world*.[28]

We can now conclude that the notion of *world-entry* has to do with Dasein's transcending capacity. This has a bearing on the distinction between 'world' and 'nature'. 'Nature' exists independently of human existence—of Dasein, but as soon as there is a Dasein, an actual human existence integrating itself in nature, it (nature) can be seen as the context of the world. The things and objects of nature will, on the occasion when the Dasein discovers them through its capacity to transcend, become part of the world of that specific Dasein; and thus they are points of world-entry. The logical distinction between nature and world still re-mains.

The easiest way to approach this distinction is to talk about nature as world whenever it is related to Dasein. Considered as entities Daseins, because of their factual existence, are part of nature in the particular way of *being-in-the-world*. In this capacity they are, however, not extant entities.[29] Transcendence makes Dasein

---

[25] Cf. Heidegger, 1984, pp 161–162.

[26] Heidegger, 1984, p 162.

[27] Heidegger, 1984, pp 165–166. I have modified the translation by using the word 'entities' instead of 'beings'.

[28] Cf. Heidegger, 1984, p 166. See also Hopkins, 1993, pp 139–141.

[29] The term 'extant' recurs throughout this chapter. It is used to identify ordinary physical substances understood as objects of the world. They are another kind of entity than the existing entities, the Daseins. Cf. Okrent, 1988, p 20f.

discover and manifest the being of entities as they are. Does this mean that transcendence relates to intentionality? There are formulations in Heidegger's discussions which also occur in relation to intentionality. An example is the phrase "that towards which".

He says: "Transcendence, being-in-the-world, is never to be equated and identified with intentionality",[30] but also: "... what has to be seen is that it is precisely intentionality and nothing else in which *transcendence* consists".[31] And further:

> ... the intentional constitution of the Dasein's comportments is precisely the *ontological condition of the possibility of every and any transcendence*. ... Intentionality is the ratio cognoscendi of transcendence. Transcendence is the ratio essendi of intentionality in its diverse modes.[32]

In my opinion these statements can only be juxtaposed by referring to Heidegger's notion of 'temporality' in relation to the notion of 'freedom'. This also provides a possible answer to our question concerning the meaning of the 'ground'.

Dasein's Freedom Manifested through Transcendence and Temporality

When Heidegger says that the Dasein is free, it must be interpreted in relation to the flow of possible choices with which the Dasein is always confronted. The leading principle is that as Dasein I am always free to make the necessary choices required in each particular situation. This has nothing to do with selfishness or egocentrism, but as he puts it:

> ... only because Dasein as such, as free, applies itself for itself, is Dasein essentially such that in each case it factically stands before the choice of how it should, in a particular case, in the ontic-existentiell sense, apply itself for others and for itself.[33]

For the Dasein to be taken in its ontic-existentiell sense—that is when a Dasein finds itself as an individual existence in a specific situation—it has, according to Heidegger, to be involved in the pre-ontological understanding of entities, i.e., in a non-theoretical understanding of the status of entities. As has been suggested by Burt Hopkins:

> Heidegger further unfolds this pre-ontological essential determination of Dasein, whereby it always understands itself from its existence, in terms of possibilities of itself which it has either chosen, found itself involved in, or already grown into. He calls the understanding of existence which manages itself in this way 'existentiell' (*existenziell*). The question of existence is accordingly understood by Heidegger to be an ontical affair for Dasein.[34]

---

[30] Heidegger, 1984, p 168.
[31] Heidegger, 1982, p 63.
[32] Heidegger, 1982, p 65.
[33] Heidegger, 1984, p 196.
[34] Hopkins, 1993, p 87.

This *existentiell* understanding of Dasein as an entity on the ontic level does not involve an inquiry into what constitutes its, or other entities', 'being'. By using the term 'existentiell' I here refer to singular, individual, human choices and experiences. It belongs to the apophantic investigation that deals with possible ways to be, in the sense of different roles that we can play. When we are trying to come to terms with our own existence, i.e., with what it means to be Dasein, we relate to these previous, individual, existentiell, understandings through 'historicity', because we have the possibility to compare our own situations with those of others; we can mirror ourselves against other people's life-experiences. In this process existentiell experiences can be conceived of as expressions of existentials by providing existential understanding.

The unfolding of the ontological structures which constitute existence is, according to Heidegger, a theoretical investigation into the *existentials* of existence. The investigation provides 'ontological-existential' understanding. Transcendence is primarily manifested to the 'ontic-existentiell' understanding because it is first of all through transcendence that we are given necessary access to entities in general. It is only when an entity has been made manifest that we can enter into an ontological-existential analysis and this is only possible because of Dasein's *being-in-the-world*.

As I have tried to indicate above, *being-in-the-world* is Dasein's fundamental way of being. This is only possible through *Dasein's* capacity to transcend, which belongs to the essence of Dasein. It is only in this capacity Dasein can exist in a world, because this capacity enables the possibility of creating a world in which it necessarily dwells. Consequently, *being-in-the-world* implies the possibility of transcending the world. 'World-entry' requires an understanding of transcendence as temporality,[35] because entering into the world means becoming temporalized. Entities may thus be understood and determined as intra-temporal.[36]

Summing up, I suggest the following interpretation. Heidegger uses the notion of 'transcendence' for the purpose of expounding what he regards as the essence of 'ground'. Transcendence is described in its metaphysical aspect, which is declared to belong to the constitution of Dasein, i.e., to its 'being'. This means that Dasein may be understood as the creator of its own world, which in turn is closely related to Heidegger's use of the notion of temporality. Dasein becomes manifest in our most fundamental way of existing; that is by *being-in-the-world*. In this mode of being we exist in a manner in which we as Daseins are always directed toward something and at the same time also exist in a manner of continuous temporalization.

As I pointed out, 'freedom' means understanding ourselves as capable of making choices. This freedom springs out of our *capacity-to-be*—which is also a *capacity-to-be-with*. Freedom, therefore, always points at *being-with*. This interpretation helps to explain the phrase: "Transcendence is ... the primordial constitution of the *subjectivity* of a subject".[37] It is only through the capacity to tran-

---

[35] Heidegger, 1984, p 210.
[36] Heidegger, 1984, p 212.
[37] Heidegger, 1984, p 165.

scend that Dasein can reflect on itself and relate to other entities. This enables the capacity-to-be to make choices: "Only through freedom, only a free being can, as transcending, understand being—and it must do so in order to exist as such, i.e., to be 'among' and 'with' beings".[38]

In defining 'ground' as essentially belonging to 'being' by pointing out that the first principal statement of logic in its ontological sense is also a statement of ground, Heidegger returned to Greek philosophers like Parmenides, Heraclitus, Plato and Aristotle and to Greek words like ἀλήθεια and λόγος. The reason was Heidegger's finding in Greek ontology, expressed through the words *phusis*, *aletheia* and *logos*, a *naive* ontology founded on everyday experience.[39] 'Being' is the ground for entities and is, among other ways, uncovered through *logos*.[40]

Logos is a recurrent notion in Heidegger's thinking. It is found in his discourses on logic and metaphysics as well as in his reconstruction of the word 'phenomenology'. He makes a special point of the fact that the term 'phenomenology' is a compound of the two Greek words φαινόμενον and λόγος. He follows Aristotle's use of the term 'logos' as primarily speech, as vocal-linguistic articulation.[41] Another important aspect of the term 'logos' is that speech manifests something. Discussing Plato in *The Basic Problems of Phenomenology* he says that:

> The logos has the peculiarity of making manifest, either of uncovering or of disclosing something, ... As basic comportment of the psuche, the logos is an aletheuein, a making-manifest, ... ancient philosophy orients its ontology to the logos and it could be said with a certain propriety that ancient ontology is a logic of being.[42]

Heidegger develops his ontology against the background of Greek philosophy and the ones of Leibniz and Kant. There are, though, different opinions among scholars on Heidegger's philosophy of what sort of dependence this background plays for him.[43] For our purpose it is important to identify what Heidegger means by 'logos' as a making-manifest in relation to 'being' and the phenomenon.

The Phenomenon

A brief definition of Heidegger's understanding of 'phenomenon' is *"that which shows itself in itself"*.[44] This definition may seem very trivial, but it is not. I propose the following twofold clarification.

Firstly, in relation to Dasein 'being' is the foundation, i.e., it is that which makes an entity (Dasein) exist. Secondly, in relation to things and objects (extant entities), 'being' refers to the establishing of concepts [Begriffe]. I will try to illustrate this by means of Heidegger's delicate use of words. To be able to grasp [greifen] anything at all, we have to be equipped with what Heidegger calls a 'pre-

---

[38] Heidegger, 1984, p 189.
[39] Taminiaux, 1991, p 102f. Cf. footnote 16 above.
[40] Okrent, 1988, p 228.
[41] Heidegger, 1984, p 22f.
[42] Heidegger, 1982, p 73.
[43] See articles by Mark Okrent and Richart Rorty in Dreyfus and Hall 1993, Ch. 7 and 11.
[44] Cf. Heidegger, 1993b, p 51.

conception' [Vorgriff]. By putting what is to be grasped [begreifen] in relation to the network of concepts, i.e., our pre-conceptions, we may comprehend the meaning of that which we are confronted with. Thus, what has been grasped, in the sense of being understood [begreifen], has become a concept [Begriff] which we can use.

The section in *Sein und Zeit* treating the concept [Begriff] of 'phenomenon', gives the reader an insight in Heidegger's way of interpreting the Greek roots of his own notions. The following observations are important for our discussion:

– according to Heidegger the Greek word φαινόμενα, the phenomena, was sometimes treated by the Greeks as synonymous with τὰ ὄντα, entities.
– entities may show themselves differently depending on the form of access open to us.
– entities might show themselves as they are in reality, i.e., in actuality, but they can also fail to do so. In such cases we are only dealing with 'semblances' [Schein].

Thus the notion of phenomenon is in its original sense ambiguous. On the one hand, it is that which shows itself as it really is, and on the other hand it includes the aspect of semblance [Schein]. But:

> When φαινόμενον signifies 'semblance', the primordial signification (the phenomenon as the manifest) is already included as that upon which the second signification is founded.[45]

Heidegger stipulates as the definition of the phenomenon its original meaning and designates its sense of semblance as belonging to its individual modification.[46] By the individual modification of the phenomenon is meant each phenomenon's possible, individual variation as far as extant entities, *non-Daseins*, as phenomena are concerned.

I have pointed out above (Ch. 2) Husserl's understanding of the phenomenon as *Erscheinung*, appearance. Heidegger makes a clear distinction between the phenomenon and appearance, including what he calls 'mere appearance'.[47] The reason is this:

> Thus appearance, as the appearance 'of something', does *not* mean showing-itself; it means rather the announcing-itself by ... something which does not show itself, but which announces itself through something which does show itself.[48]

Appearance is different from semblance since, according to Heidegger, appearance is neither a *not-showing-itself* nor a pretence while semblance does at least pretend to show itself. Both notions are in different ways founded on phenomenon. A phenomenon, that which shows itself in its showing, is in that sense a possible event through which something can be found, i.e., uncovered. The ap-

[45] Heidegger, 1993b, p 51.
[46] Cf. Hopkins, 1993, p 90f.
[47] Heidegger, 1993b, p 51f.
[48] Heidegger, 1993b, p 52.

54

pearance, in turn, is a referential relationship by means of the act of announcing [meldend] something. But this act can only achieve its function as appearence if there is a phenomenon available.[49] Heidegger is here first of all trying to differentiate his understanding of the phenomenon from that of Kant. Kant understood phenomenon as *Erscheinung*; as the appearance of the thing in itself [das Ding an sich]. It is this appearance which is observable and thus identifiable through empirical investigations. For Heidegger, the phenomenon cannot reveal itself or uncover itself by means of empirical investigation.

The differentiation between 'phenomenon' and 'appearance' also implies a position different from that of Husserl. Although there are obvious similarities between Husserl's and Heidegger's understandings of the notion of the phenomenon as that which shows itself, there are also obvious differences. The most fundamental one is that for Husserl phenomenon is founded on the intentional act as the correspondence between intentio and intentum, and in this sense phenomenon is a conscious content, while for Heidegger the phenomenon is not primarily a conscious content, but is to be discovered through people's dwelling in the world. Thus it is connected to the Da-Sein.

By investigating Heidegger's explorations of the notions of phenomenon and logos, I find myself thrown back on the definition of phenomenon as 'that which shows itself'. This phrase is connected to 'being' and its meaning can only be discovered through the analysis of Dasein. However, Heidegger's view is still rather unclear. Can it be further clarified by treating his phenomenology as a non-epistemological project?

When discussing Husserl it became clear that his phenomenology is founded on an epistemological challenge, i.e., on the quest for absolute certitude. Heidegger seems to focus his phenomenology differently. He wants to go beyond Husserl's phenomenology in the sense of having its locus in consciousness and its intentional structures.[50] Because of his view that Husserl does not relate his phenomenology to the hermeneutics of Dasein, Heidegger regards Husserl's use of the term 'phenomenon' as well as 'phenomenology' as unoriginal. Husserl does not relate either notion to the fundamental ontology of 'being'. To be able to interpret the significance of Heidegger's notion of phenomenon, we must turn our focus on his notion of Dasein and the analysis thereof.

The Phenomenological Method as an Analysis of Dasein

The notion of Dasein holds the same central position in Heidegger's philosophy as does the one of 'being'. We must now try to identify what 'Dasein' stands for.

To enter into an authentic [eigentlich] understanding of ourselves and of the surrounding world we must, according to Heidegger, start by asking about our own being. However, we cannot gain direct access to the 'being' as such; it must be done by asking about our own unique human existence. Every existing human

---

[49] Heidegger, 1993b, p 53. Cf. Hopkins, 1993, p 91.
[50] Hopkins, 1993, p 158.

being is through the word 'is' presented to themselves and to others as an entity [Seiendes]. Every kind of entity carries its own specific mode of being [Seinsmodus] as the ground defined by everyone's different essential constitution as beings.[51] For human beings, this specific mode of 'being', uniquely expressed through humanity, is defined by Heidegger as *Existenz*. Compared to other entities, human beings have a unique opportunity to reflect on their own existence. By the notion of Dasein, Heidegger wants to describe the everyday existence of human beings.[52]

Dasein is not to be identified as a conscious subject. Even so, every human being, as a conscious subject, can reflect on their relation *to* their own unique 'being'. This is expressed by the writing of the notion as *Da-sein*. The *Da*, which indicates a possible here/there relationship, carries a temporal aspect which might explain the following statement by Heidegger: "In everydayness Dasein is not that Being that *I* am. Rather the everydayness of Dasein is that Being that *one* is. And Dasein, accordingly, is the time in which *one* is with one another: 'one's' time."[53]

This can be further qualified by pointing at the fact that *being-in-the-world* always indicates a spatial relation to the surrounding Daseins—i.e., other human beings—as well as to extant things, to the objects etc. that make up our world. Thus the 'there' [Da] also carries a spatial aspect. In §28 of *Sein und Zeit*, Heidegger continues: "'Here' and 'yonder' are possible only in a 'there'—that is to say, only if there is an entity which has made a disclosure of spatiality as the Being of the 'there'."[54]

We now have two important factors which will lead us further into Heidegger's notions of 'temporality' and 'intentionality', i.e., the expression of 'another one's time' and of 'spatiality'.

The Notion of 'Time'

As we shall see, the notion of time is of fundamental importance in Heidegger's thinking. Here I will concentrate on 'time' in relation to 'historicity' [Geschichtlichkeit].

On the question of what time is, Heidegger writes:

> ... what matters in the question concerning time is attaining an answer in terms of which the various ways of being temporal become comprehensible ...[55]

Heidegger here indicates that human beings, described as Daseins, exist in time in some distinctive way. Following this line, he identifies the ontological characteristics of Dasein:[56]

---

[51] Heidegger, 1993b, p 26f.
[52] Dreyfus, 1991, p 13.
[53] Heidegger, 1992b, p 17E.
[54] Heidegger, 1993b, p 171. See also Heidegger, 1972, p 132.
[55] Heidegger, 1992b, p 7E.
[56] For the following, cf. Heidegger, 1992b, pp 7E–11E.

- as an entity characterized as *being-in-the-world*,
- as dealing with the world as performance, contemplation, investigation etc.,
- as 'care'[Sorge], i.e., *being-in-the-world* as *being-with-one-another* as well as *being-for-one-another*,
- as communication by *speaking* to one another,
- as the uniqueness of the 'I *am*' as constitutive for Dasein, i.e., Dasein is always and in each case my own,
- as concern for the *being* of Dasein, which is always an existence in the world, and when speaking of the world this includes Dasein's speaking about itself,
- as becoming aware of itself in a *Da* (here/there) through whatever it is dealing with,
- as I am with the other people in the same way as they are. Dasein is thus based on a kind of mutual, responsible relationships of self-understandings, but this must never mean that I am the Other,
- as its way of *being-in-the-world*. Dasein's 'being' cannot be grasped by contemplation, it can only be grasped through experience, just by '*being it*'.

According to Heidegger we can relate to time in different ways. By always connecting Dasein to the present in a static sense, we fail to reach insight into Dasein as 'temporality'. The crucial questions of 'how' and 'when' have to be put in such ways that Dasein can always explain itself as self-transcending. This means that Dasein always exists in the present in an intermediate state between the past, the present, and the future. It is through Dasein as temporality that we can find an entry into Heidegger's understanding of history [Geschichte] and into history seen in its aspect of historicity [Geschichtlichkeit], i.e., as a means for Dasein to choose ways of handling existentiell situations.

By understanding history as a collection of events and facts of the past, I may use history in a scholarly way. In this way history does not present my own Dasein with opportunities of disclosing its 'being' as the basis for that specific entity. History in this sense can be seen as events in time. Time in history and time in mathematics and physics etc. must be seen in their scientific context, where there are different concepts of time with different functions.

For the human *Dasein,* time and history must be grasped in their historicity. I suggest that we interpret the notion of *historicity* as a culture's collective memory, which is open to us in forms of infinite possibilities, some of them recorded as actual existentiell choices and experiences. Heidegger writes:

> The past remains closed off from any present so long as such a present, Dasein, is not itself historical. Dasein, however, is in itself historical in so far as it is its possibility. In being futural Dasein is its past; it comes back to it in the 'how'. ... The past—experienced as authentic historicity—is anything but what is past. It is something to which I can return again and again.[57]

[57] Heidegger, 1992b, p 19E . The term 'authentic' is in my opinion an unfortunate translation of the German word 'eigentlich' which more directly links up with the Dasein as always my own [eigen]. 'Authentic' can lead to interpretations that in one way or another have a value connotation. As far as my own interpretation of Heidegger is correct, the 'eigentlich'/'uneigentlich' distinction carries no value. They only indicate possibilities of how to understand ourselves differently.

"The past ... is anything but the past" has to be seen against the idea of *Geschicht-lichkeit*, historicity. Heidegger's view is that we are always in the past, in the sense that we always have to recapture previous experiences in order to be able to make successful choices, i.e., that the future outcome of a choice will provide us with authentic self-understanding.

The Notion of Temporality

The quotation above gives the background to Heidegger's statement that Dasein is time by always being in time, in one way or the other. He qualifies this by stating that Dasein is not time itself but rather 'temporality' [Zeitlichkeit].[58] In *Sein und Zeit*, he seems to modify his view on temporality by pointing out temporality as the 'meaning' [Sinn] of the 'being' of the entity known as Dasein.[59] He disting-uishes between two different modes of Dasein's relation to the surrounding world, which in relation to understanding [Verstehen] is revealed as authenticity [Ei-gentlichkeit] or inauthenticity [Uneigentlichkeit].

For the entity known as Dasein, temporality is said to be the condition of all understandings of 'being'. Dasein is occupied with '*its own ability to be*',[60] which is expressed through the three characteristics of temporality: expectation, reten-tion and making present.[61] They correspond to the three 'ecstases' of temporality: *Zukunft*, *Gewesenheit* and *Gegenwart*:

> We ... call future, past and present the three *ecstases* of temporality; they belong together intrinsically with co-equal originality. ...The term 'ecstatic' has nothing to do with ecstatic states of mind ... The common Greek expression ekstatikon means stepping-outside-self. It is affiliated with the term 'existence'. It is with this ecstatic character that we interpret existence, ... In its ecstatic character, temporality is the condition of the constitution of the Dasein's being.[62]

According to Heidegger, the ecstase's future and past carry an aspect of the present. The future is conceived of in terms of expectations, i.e., as something to come or to happen later. When an action is planned, its outcome in terms of expected results belongs to the present. The past also belongs to the present inas-much as memories and experiences are present, even though the specific act be-longs to the past. When we express this, we do so in terms of *now*. Thus when we say 'later', 'before' and 'now', we are talking about time for something to hap-pen. Expressing ourselves in this way, we also understand what others express by their use of these words. This can create an opportunity for us to understand the existentiell situations of others as individual Daseins *being-in-the-world*. And since temporality, and the way it is expressed, is a condition for all human beings, it is also an existential characteristic of being-in the-world.

Against this background I want to return to the notion of historicity/historical-

---

[58] Heidegger, 1992b, p 20E.
[59] Heidegger, 1993b, p 38. Cf. Okrent, 1988, p 191f.
[60] Heidegger, 1982, p 276.
[61] Taminiaux, 1991, p 90.
[62] Heidegger, 1982, p 267.

ity. History can be said to function as a database of stored human experiences. According to Heidegger, we have the possibility of mirroring our own Dasein against these *existentiell* experiences of other people. I think it is appropriate to interpret this option as an 'existential possibility', which will also clarify further the notion of Geschichtlichkeit.

I shall now present a preliminary mapping out of Heidegger's view on the conditions for our human existence [Existenz]. This will lead us to an understanding of phenomena at large and of existential phenomena in particular.

Dasein's Fundamental Condition as Being-in-the-World

Heidegger's notion of the world must be seen in relation to Dasein's existing in relationships. This is expressed by the notion of *being-in-the-world*.

As previously mentioned, Dasein is an entity, but it is distinguished from other entities by its ability to reflect on its own 'being'.[63] In other words, I have an opportunity to relate to myself and to others, both human beings and things, through understanding [Verstehen]. This means for example that by reflecting on other people's solutions to life-situations similar to any particular one that I myself may be facing, I am given an opportunity to interpret my own life-situation and thus to gain an authentic self-understanding, irrespective of whether or not these solutions have been successful.

The distinguishing ontic quality of Dasein is the opening up [erschlossen] of its own 'being'.[64] Entities are described as ontic in Heidegger's thinking. And ways of being are described as ontological.[65]

The being towards which the Dasein can and always does conduct itself in one way or another is called existence [Existenz] by Heidegger.[66] To exist is to be selfinterpreting. Only Dasein, with its ability to reflect on its own being as *Zu-sein* possesses this particular existence. The notion of *Zu-sein* indicates that the *Dasein* adopts itself towards other entities.[67] Since Dasein always lives within temporality which is the constitutive condition for Dasein's 'being', its understanding of *being-in-the-world* is twofold. It is an existentiell understanding: temporality[68] is expressed in terms of the three 'exstases': past, present and future. It is also an understanding of other entities that exist, not in terms of *Existenz* but as being at hand.[69]

Dasein's understanding of its own 'being', as well as of other extant entities, is not possible without its existence [Existenz] *being-in-the-world*.[70] This means that every form of understanding is founded on this manner of existing. *Being-in-the-world* is thus a necessary condition for understanding in general. Without

---

[63] Heidegger, 1993b, p 32. Cf. p 27 n1.
[64] Heidegger, 1993b, p 32f.
[65] Dreyfus, 1991, p 20.
[66] Dreyfus, 1991, p 14f. Cf. Heidegger, 1993b, p 32.
[67] Cf. Heidegger, 1982, p 318f.
[68] Heidegger, 1982, §20, pp 279–286.
[69] Okrent, 1988, pp 39–41. Cf. Heidegger, 1993b, p 67f .
[70] Heidegger, 1982, p 164.

being-in-the-world there is no Dasein present, and there is nothing to relate to since there is nobody to understand, and therefore there is no self-understanding.

Before entering into the discussion on Heidegger's view on understanding, let me briefly sum up some central points.

(a) Phenomenology as philosophy is first of all ontology because of its focus on the question of *being*.

(b) 'Being' is the principle basis for existence [Existenz].

(c) There is a difference between 'being' and 'entities'. It can be expressed as the difference between facts and their ground. Heidegger calls it the 'ontological difference'.

(d) Heidegger's notion of phenomenon has to do with 'being', while Husserl's notion refers to considerations about entities.

(e) Human beings are in this world in the sense of Dasein.

(f) 'Being' is the foundation for the entity of Dasein.

(g) Dasein always lives in 'temporality'.

(h) Temporality is characterized by its three 'ecstases': the future, the past, and the present.

(i) Through its ecstatic character, temporality is the condition for the constitution of Dasein's 'being'.

(j) Dasein exists in the manner of *being-in-the-world*.

(k) Self-interpretation is the necessary condition for Dasein's existence [Existenz].

(l) Self-interpretation is Dasein's distinguishing ontic quality. By *being-in-the-world*, Dasein's ontic significance is being ontological. This constitutes the 'ontological difference' between 'being' and 'entities'.

Existentiell Understanding as Authentic or Inauthentic

As I have indicated above, the terms 'authentic' and 'inauthentic' must not be used as equivalent to the adjectives 'right' and 'wrong', 'good' and 'bad'. Heidegger uses this terminology to describe two possible ways of understanding—two possibilities of Dasein's *being-in-the-world*. The way we ought to interpret authenticity [Eigentlichkeit] and inauthenticity [Uneigentlichkeit] is clearly formulated in *Being and Time*:

> As modes of Being, *authenticity* and *inauthenticity* (these expressions have been chosen terminologically in a strict sense) are both grounded in the fact that any Dasein whatsoever is characterized by mineness.[71]

The *mineness* [Jemeinigkeit] means that Dasein is a Self in its own right.[72] Through the mineness we have the possibility of self-understanding, both in the manner of authenticity and of inauthenticity. To be a self, in the sense of being-one's-own, means to choose oneself authentically.

[71] Heidegger, 1993b, p 68.
[72] Taminiaux, 1991, p 88. Cf. Heidegger, 1982, p 170. Taminiaux uses the term 'ownness' as equivalent to being-one's-own, the translation of the expression used by Heidegger.

The meaning of self-understanding might be easier to grasp if it is interpreted in terms of self-identification. According to Heidegger, we have lost ourselves when we identify ourselves in everyday life with things or with other people to the extent that we reduce ourselves to become copies of others. Then we understand ourselves inauthentically.[73] Inauthentic self-understanding means that we are not our own. It does not mean that this self-understanding should be ascribed a negative value. It rather reflects our most common way of existing:

> The Dasein's average understanding of itself takes the self as in-authentic. ... The genuine, actual, though inauthentic understanding of the self takes place in such a way that this self, the self of our thoughtlessly random, common, everyday existence, 'reflects' itself to itself from out of that to which it has given itself over.[74]

Inauthentic self-understanding results from alienation although we must distinguish between Heidegger's notion of alienation from that of Karl Marx. For Karl Marx, alienation concerns the working-process. The labourers identify themselves fully with the product during the process of production, but the alienation results from the fact that the means of production as well as the final product belong to somebody else. For Heidegger—who like Marx takes Hegel's notion of alienation as his point of departure—alienation means, in particular, estrangement from oneself. This alienation puts an end to Dasein's authenticity and to its possibility of being-one's-own by forcing Dasein into its in-authenticity.[75] By identifying myself totally with the other, by copying another's life, I lose at least the possibility to fail in an authentic way, both with regard to my existential understanding of what it is to be Dasein, and to my existentiell understanding of my own way of being what I am. Self-understanding should not, says Heidegger, be formally equated with a reflected ego-experience, since the latter does not reflect the necessary *to-be-with*, which expresses the responsibility of *being-in-the-world*; nor does it automatically lead to self-understanding. When existentiell self-understanding is situation-dependent, it varies in every existentiell situation with the mode of Dasein's basic forms of authenticity and inauthenticity.[76]

By always *being-in-the-world*, I can, as Dasein, achieve an understanding of myself in two ways. First we can understand our *being-in-the-world* as an existentiell understanding, founded in temporality. By means of the existentiell understanding we can relate our own way of 'being' to that of other people and we can compare ours with theirs. Secondly, this can provide existential understanding in which the Dasein understands itself in its innermost capacity of 'being', which is the capacity to be me with others.

I will try to put this as simply as possible. In the context of existentiell understanding the term 'resoluteness' is used to describe authentic understanding. Resoluteness, or maybe we could say 'choice', is used by Heidegger to describe

---

[73] Heidegger, 1982, p 160.
[74] Heidegger, 1982, p 160f.
[75] Heidegger, 1993b, p 222.
[76] Heidegger, 1982, p 175.

throwing oneself into the unknown, the existentiell option so delicately pin-pointed by Kierkegaard in the phrase: *the leap of faith.*

Throughout my existence, I am always confronted with situations that require the making of choices. By taking into account experiences from the past, either my own or other people's, I can make a decision, a choice, based on experience, and thus I may have expectations for the future. This is the central idea in Heidegger's formulation:

> In resoluteness the Dasein understands itself from its own most peculiar can-be. Understanding is primarily futural, for it comes toward itself from its chosen possi-bility of itself. ... In resoluteness, that is, ... in this coming-toward-itself from its own most peculiar possibility, the Dasein comes back to that which it is and takes itself over as the being that it is. ... The temporal mode in which it is as and what it *was* we call ... *repetition.* ... In the ecstatic unity of *repetitive self-precedence*, in this past and future, there lies a specific present.[77]

Phenomenology of Perception

I now return to the important distinction:

> World is only, if, and as long a Dasein exists. Nature can also be when no Dasein exists. ... Nature can also be without there being a world, without a Dasein existing.[78]

The notion of 'world' requires a Dasein knowing about it. This knowledge of the world presupposes Dasein's *being-in-the-world*, which is a necessary condition for all possible understanding. By *being-in-the-world*, 'nature' is available for Dasein as the extant sum of things and entities. Of these entities some are essen-tially functional by determination, whilst others are not.

Aesthetic and natural objects that are characterized as non-functional are con-sidered by Heidegger to have a natural determination. These entitites are the ones that are called *extant*. They are 'present-at-hand' [vorhanden].[79] Nature is not the world in the sense of Dasein's recognized dwelling-place. There is no Dasein present to know, neither to understand how to relate to nature, nor how to use it functionally. This means that there are extant things, especially of natural objects, that exist independent of Daseins.

Being-in-the-world means for a Dasein to be *with* and *among* other entities and things. From among all the extant things, we know some of them but we might not understand them. Not to understand is, for Heidegger, to be unfamiliar with function and usage. Unless the extant things become familiar to the Dasein, we do not know how to deal with them appropriately.[80] Here we find the difference between extant entities present-at-hand [vorhanden], and extant entities ready-to-hand [zuhanden]. The term 'zuhanden' has to do with our pragmatic dealing with

[77] Heidegger, 1982, p 287. This claim will be of significance for us in the analysis of van der Leeuw's understanding and use of the notion of repetition.
[78] Heidegger, 1982, p 170, 175.
[79] Cf. Okrent, 1988, p 74.
[80] Heidegger, 1982, p 304.

entities. These entities are indicated by Heidegger by the term 'equipment' [Zeug]. They belong to the ontological category of 'readiness-to-hand' [Zuhandenheit]. Things called 'equipment' are determined by a context of use. Writing, for example, requires a certain kind of equipment like pen and paper. A particular thing is not an equipment in itself.[81]

Items of equipment are distinguished, by Heidegger, from entities encountered as being 'presence-at-hand' [Vorhandenheit].[82] The latter shows itself "in the different sort of possibility the extant is understood to have insofar as it is extant".[83] These different possibilities have to do with varieties of praxis.

These possibilities appear as options in our dealing with entities. Dealing with is, in Heidegger's terminology, equivalent to 'commerce'. Optional commerce, or dealing with extant things, is grasping their 'equipmental contexture'. This involves a Dasein's understanding of a particular entity. When the 'whatness', i.e., the equipmental contexture, is grasped so that its functionality is understood, and when it is available, Heidegger defines it as 'handiness'. That which gets demonstrated in use is the thing as a tool. Thus it is made present to the Dasein. Through handiness commerce with entities becomes possible. "Handiness formally implies praesens, presence [Anwesenheit], but a praesens of a particular sort."[84] Handiness is distinguished from the 'at hand' [vorhanden]. When an extant thing is not available, not 'at hand', it does not mean that it is non-'being'. It is simply not available, in the sense of having no known 'equipmental role'.

Now, the way something is understood in its functionality requires that its 'being', in this sense its 'reference' [Bedeutung], is uncovered. According to Heidegger, this uncovering is performed through perception, and means the uncovering of the truth of the extant thing. It makes present, in the sense of an *aletheuein,* the essential meaning of the extant entity. It is important to underline that it is the essential meaning of the extant entity that is discovered, not just the meaning it has for me. Let us take the engine of a car as an example. When its essential meaning is made manifest through perception and interpretation, the meaning of the car engine can be found in its working in accordance with its design. It functions according to its equipmental structure as a whole.

Heidegger's notion of perception is central in his phenomenology. Jacques Taminiaux sums up Heidegger's views in four points:

> 1. perception is an intentional comportment whose specific orientation is turned toward something *vorhanden*, something present-at-hand; 2. this comportment is intrinsically uncovering, ... in its very orientation it is open to the uncovered *vorhanden*; 3. this uncoveredness takes place in the light of Being, ... in the light of presence-at-hand (*Vorhandenheit*) as the Being always already unveiled of the present-at-hand entities; 4. the light in which the uncoveredness occurs is the light of the ontological difference ...[85]

---

[81] Dreyfus, 1991, p 62f.
[82] Cf. Fell, 1993, p 65.
[83] Okrent, 1988, p 80.
[84] Okrent, 1988, p 212. Okrent here quotes *The Basic Problems of Phenomenology*.
[85] Taminiaux, 1991, p 89.

This quotation needs some explanation. First of all, it is necessary to interpret the term 'being' as it occurs in the text. In my opinion Taminiaux here refers to the uncovering of the true meaning of an object or a thing (the case of the car engine above). Heidegger also talks about the uncovering of 'being' in relation to entities of this kind, but there is a difference between the 'being' of Daseins and of extant entities. The being of a thing is basically to be seen in the light of praxis, i.e., of Dasein's dealing with it, while the 'being' of Daseins refers to existence. In my opinion, point 4 above should be understood against this background.

One idea of perception that Heidegger wants to avoid is the naive, natural viewing of things. The mistake in this understanding of perception lies in the relationship between a subject, present-at-hand, and an observed object/thing that is also present-at-hand. The improper intentional relation is described as: "... an extant relation between two things extant, a psychical subject and a physical object".[86] The proper intentional relation does not arise by the addition of an object to a subject., but "... the subject is structured intentionally within itself. As subject it is directed toward ...".[87] This directedness of the Dasein as subject is interpreted in terms of Dasein's fundamental condition of *being-in-the-world*.

If the intentional relation would only arise with the additional relation between a psychical subject and an extant physical object, then dreams, fantasies, hallucinations, etc. would not be possible. Husserl solved this problem by means of talking about intentional experiences of intentional inexistence, i.e., about intentional experiences where the intentional object, the 'intentum', cannot be proven as existing extra-mentally.[88] According to Husserl religious experiences of God are examples of these kinds of intentional experiences.

In relation to the most elementary (i.e., basic, not elementary in a pejorative sense) form of perception, which is the immediate vision in the twinkle of an eye, the act of perception is first a consideration of something *vorhanden, present-at-hand*. This 'present-at-hand' is in turn founded on, and thus extracted from, something which is *zuhanden, ready-to-hand*. Entities that are 'ready-to-hand' are based on functionality, i.e., on the functional totality of the surrounding world [Umwelt]. Heidegger makes the following important distinction:

> Two things are to be established: (1) being-in-the-world belongs to the concept of existence; (2) factically existent Dasein, factical being-in-the-world, is always already being-with intraworldly entities. To factical being-in-the-world there always belongs a being-with intraworldly entities. ... Intraworldliness belongs to the being of the extant, nature, *not* as a determination of its being, but as a *possible* determination, and one that is necessary for the possibility of the uncoverability of nature.[89]

Thus anything *zuhanden* and *vorhanden* is something intraworldly, the uncoveredness of which presupposes both the world and the unveiling of the world. The

---

[86] Heidegger, 1982, p 60.
[87] Heidegger, 1982, p 60.
[88] Husserl, 1970b, vol 2, p 596.
[89] Heidegger, 1982, p 168f. I have modified the translation through my use of the word 'entities' instead of 'beings'.

term 'intraworldly' relates to entities with which we can deal practically, which means that they are made possible and framed by the totality of references or of significant meanings in the world.[90] This world is made up by Dasein through its relationships to its surroundings. As Heidegger concludes:

> To intentionality, as comportment towards entities, there always belongs an *understanding of the being* of those entities [intentum] to which the intentio [a specific Dasein] refers ... this understanding of the being of entities is connected with the *understanding of world*, which is the presupposition for the experience of an intraworldly entity.[91]

The Notion of Intentionality

We have already touched on Heidegger's use of the notion of intentionality in relation to perception. In order to clarify his position in comparison to Husserl's view, let us highlight some important aspects based on his critique of Husserl's notion of 'intentionality'.

This problem has been extensively dealt with by Burt C. Hopkins in his work *Intentionality in Husserl and Heidegger*. I will only discuss the problems of 'objectivizing' and 'subjectivizing' intentionality. These two problems of Husserl's notion of intentionality will be important for our discussion of the possibility of grasping phenomena by means of recollection and repetition, and particularly for our discussion of Gerardus van der Leeuw's idea of a phenomenology of religion as a method by which we can re-experience religious experiences and thus re-experience the intentional relation of religious phenomena. The problem will occur when we ask to what degree an original experience can be recollected and what exactly is being re-experienced.

As Heidegger understands it, erroneous 'objectivizing of intentionality' refers to the naive, natural understanding of perception which we discussed above. In such an intentional relation the perceiving subject, as well as the perceived object, are on the level of being 'present-at-hand'. Heidegger expounds this erroneous interpretation:

> The mistake lies in the fact that this interpretation takes the intentional relation to be something that at each time accrues to the subject due to the emergence of the extantness of an object.[92]

The objectivizing is thus, in my opinion, due to the misinterpretation of the 'I' as a psychological subject, and to the understanding of both the psychological subject and the physical object as being extant entities. This would mean: "If there were no physical things, then the psychological subject, without this intentional relation, would have to be extant for itself in an isolated way".[93]

---

[90] Fell, 1993, p 65.
[91] Heidegger, 1982, p 175. I have modified the translation by using the word 'entities' instead of 'beings'.
[92] Heidegger, 1982, p 60. Cf. Hopkins, 1993, p 114.
[93] Heidegger, 1982, p 60.

For Heidegger, this is an impossible thought. This is obvious when we recall what was said above about the world, the extant entities and the Dasein.

The subjectivizing of intentionality is erroneous from a different angle. Returning to Husserl we recall how intentionality was founded on 'lived experiences', in which the intentional object was given through the intentional act. Thus, intentionality can be said to belong to the subject in the way that the *intentio* and *intentum* are understood in terms of an ego's experiences. Intentional self-directing towards the intentional object therefore seems to belong to the subjective sphere.[94] Heidegger responds to this misinterpretation by pointing to the fact that the question of how the subjective, intentional experience can relate to something objectively present, is erroneously formulated. Therefore we cannot:

> ... and must not ask how the inner intentional experience arrives at an outside. I cannot and must not put the question in that way because intentional comportment itself as such orients itself toward the extant. ... It follows from this that intentionality must not be misinterpreted on the basis of an arbitrary concept of the subject and ego and subjective sphere ... we shall in the future no longer speak of a subject, of a subjective sphere, but shall understand the being to whom intentional comportments belong as *Dasein*, ...[95]

Against an erroneous objectivizing of intentionality, we must, according to Heidegger, state that intentionality is not a relation between an extant subject and object, but "a structure that constitutes the *comportmental character* of the Dasein's behavior".[96] Against an erroneous 'subjectivizing of intentionality', it must be made clear that the intentional structure of comportments is not something immanent to the subject. "... rather, the intentional constitution of the Dasein's comportments is precisely the *ontological condition of the possibility of every and any transcendence*."[97]

The Dasein's necessary condition for all possible understanding is, as we have seen, constituted by its *being-in-the-world*. And it is only through Dasein's *being-in-the-world* that we can become familiar with the extant entities. Since intentionality belongs to Dasein's existence, intentionality provides the possibility for Dasein to relate it through actions, dealings etc., directed towards its own extant entity. This might explain Heidegger's view that the subject, the Dasein, is intentionally structured within itself.[98]

Hermeneutics and the Hermeneutical Situation

So far we have pointed at the three contextual dimensions of the Dasein, i.e., the spatial, the temporal, and the social dimensions. All of these belong to Dasein's existential, ontological conditions in the world. These contextual dimensions are expressed through *being-in-the-world*, and the social dimension is above all re-

---

[94] Cf. Hopkins, 1993, p 115.
[95] Heidegger, 1982, p 63f.
[96] Heidegger, 1982, p 65.
[97] Heidegger, 1982, p 65.
[98] Cf. Hopkins, 1993, p 115, § 57.

lated to Dasein's existential situation of *being-with-others*. Heidegger here expounds his hermeneutics in the light of the development of hermeneutics starting with Schleiermacher and Dilthey. Since Dilthey is of interest both in relation to Husserl and to van der Leeuw, I will set aside a section below for a discussion of his hermeneutics.

The hermeneutical character of Heidegger's phenomenology is founded on a fundamental-ontological analysis of Dasein. This analysis centres on the question of the 'being' of Dasein and the ontological difference between 'being' and entity. The investigation brings into the open[99] the 'being' of the Dasein, its meaning and its *foundational structure*. I totally agree with Dreyfus when he states:

> For Heidegger, like Wittgenstein, meaning is grounded neither in some mental reality nor in an arbitrary decision, but is based upon a form of life in which we necessarily dwell, and which, therefore, is neither immediately given nor merely a matter of choice.[100]

As has been said above, Heidegger stresses that 'being', in the sense of that which creates something else, can be expressed above all in poetic language and can be communicated through *logos* [Rede]. We name things through speech and by communication thus bring the question of 'being' into the open. In other words, *logos* has the capacity to manifest 'being' by functioning as an *aletheuein*. Heidegger formulates this in *Being and Time*:

> The λόγος of the phenomenology of Dasein has the character of ἑρμηνεύειν, through which the authentic meaning of Being, and also those basic structures of Being which Dasein itself possesses, are *made known* to Dasein's understanding of Being. The phenomenology of Dasein is a *hermeneutic* in the primordial signification of this word, where it designates this business of interpreting.[101]

In Heidegger's view, phenomenology is the method for philosophy—and 'scientific philosophy in general' is understood as 'fundamental ontology' because of its starting-point in the question of being. Therefore we must ask whether hermeneutics is a subordinate method in relation to phenomenology, or whether hermeneutics is equal to phenomenology. I would suggest that this problem can be solved by making a distinction between phenomenology as the method for unfolding the horizon against which understanding is established, while hermeneutics is the method for establishing self-understanding within this horizon.[102] Hermeneneutics can thus be said to lay open the basic structures of the possibilities for Dasein, i.e., it is the analysis of the Dasein's own possibilities for being.[103]

To be able to grasp these possibilities, a basic form of understanding that is

---

[99] The bringing into the open, or laying open is termed *Auslegung* by Heidegger and is translated into English as 'interpretation'. I think that we are to understand the term *Auslegung* in the sense of 'exposition' since what is done is an exposure of the 'being' of the Dasein.

[100] Dreyfus, 1991, p 201.

[101] Heidegger, 1993b, p 61f.

[102] The relevance of this interpretation depends on whether one understands Heidegger as using the two terms 'phenomenology' and 'hermeneutics' as equivalent or not. Cf. Føllesdal, Walløe and Elster, 1985, p 117, where it is said that Heidegger uses these terms interchangeably.

[103] Cf. Palmer, 1988, p 129f, cf. Heidegger, 1993b, p 62f.

grounded on the existential structures of Dasein is required. According to Werner Jeanrond, Heidegger seems not to be interested in all optional possibilities which the Dasein could grasp, but only in the two principal ones, because "... he wishes to distinguish between two principal possibilities, i.e. that Dasein reaches out to grasp its very own possibility of Being, or not".[104]

It follows that a Dasein's existentiell self-understanding is in principle either authentic or inauthentic. If the existentiell self-understanding is authentic, then what is experienced in it can only be meaningful because it has a bearing on the individual's life. If it is inauthentic, then what is experienced in it can be experienced as meaningful but can in fact be meaningless because it does not have a bearing on the individual's life. The possession of these possibilities is a characteristic of Dasein.[105]

Whenever we engage in an interpretative act, we do so for the purpose of achieving further understanding of the matter at hand. According to Heidegger, our interpretative activities are always preconditioned in the sense that we already have a certain knowledge or some ideas about the matter. In other words, whatever comes out of our interpretation is in some ways already understood. This presupposition is the object founded on what Heidegger calls the 'threefold pre-structure of understanding'. It is formulated in terms of 'Vorhabe', pre-possession, 'Vorsicht', fore-sight, and 'Vorgriff', pre-conception. This is explained by Mark Okrent as:

> Every interpretation, whether true ... or false, is grounded in a fore-having (that is, to interpret any entity, one must understand many others), a fore-sight (we approach the rock 'under the guidance of a view': can it be used for hammering?), and a fore-conception (in terms of some definite network of concepts, especially in the case of linguistic interpretations, or assertions), because nothing can count as an interpretation without such a fore-structure embedded in patterned practical activity.[106]

This 'fore-structure of all understanding', founded on Dasein's *being-in-the-world*, points to an important factor; namely to the circularity of the hermeneutical situation. Even though talking about the hermeneutics of texts, Peter Kosso provides a clarifying comment on circularity.

> It is **hermeneutic** in that its goal is interpretation of the text, and it is circular in open acknowledgement of the necessity of using only our available information to account for and extend our available information. It is circular because of its limited resources.[107]

An interpretation based on the quotation from Okrent could read like this: by existing under the condition of *being-in-the-world*, we are related to other Daseins and entities through the projection of a *for-the-sake-of* the world. In relation to extant entities, in the sense of *Vorhanden,* we can actually find ourselves in

---

[104] Jeanrond, 1993, p 61.
[105] Cf. Jeanrond, 1993, p 61.
[106] Okrent, 1988, p 165.
[107] Kosso, 1992, p 149.

a situation where we have no access to the proper item as something at-hand, but from previous experiences and confrontations with the extant one, we are equipped with this 'fore-structure', which can actually point out another entity at-hand, which might function as the extant thing ready-to-hand. The necessary prerequisite is that we understand the meaning of the intended thing at-hand to be a thing ready-to-hand. In relation to our own existence as relationships together with other human beings in the world, this 'fore-structure' can help us in our effort towards authentic self-understanding. The 'fore-structure' can be mirrored against the 'horizontal unity' based on the three ecstases of the past, the present, and the future; i.e., on the temporality of Dasein's being-in-the-world.

This will now bring us to the conclusion of this chapter. I will end by turning to Heidegger's notion of existentials and the existential phenomena.

Existentials and Existential Phenomena

Without any intention to anticipate my analysis of Gerardus van der Leeuw's understanding of phenomenology, I will merely underline some important points here.

In the next chapter we will see how van der Leeuw, by focusing on religions and religious life, wants to show us that, through the phenomenological analysis of religious experiences, we might reach an authentic understanding of ourselves. Religions can be said to equip us with proper answers to the fundamental questions of life, such as questions of death, guilt, awe, happiness, alienation, etc. It is my conviction that van der Leeuw's phenomenological comprehension can be illuminated by Heidegger's analysis of these so-called 'existential phenomena'.

As mentioned above, the kind of investigation is ontological, which concerns ways of being in general. Following Dreyfus, this inquiring brings forward the so-called 'existentials' and 'existential structures' using the question 'who', and it must be distinguished from the existentiell/individual question and from the question about entities, i.e., the ontic investigation. The previous ontological investigation deals with possible ways to be, being shown by the 'who'-question. Under the question 'what', the ontic investigation focuses on properties and their structures, while the ontological investigation deals with the ontological categories, i.e., with presence-at-hand and readiness-to-hand, and with their structures, such as quality and quantity. These investigations explore two forms of understanding: the *existential*, which is an elaborated understanding of what it is to be Dasein (i.e., of the ontological structures of existence), and the *existentiell* understanding, which is the individual's understanding of their own way to be what they are.[108]

That which Heidegger calls 'existentials' are necessary conditions which constitute Dasein's existence, and without which Dasein would not be. The existentials are those ontological, foundational structures that distinguish a being (as Dasein) from the surrounding, extant entities of the world. We can distinguish between two basic sorts of existentials: those characterized as mode under the

---

[108] Dreyfus, 1991, p 20.

'who'-question, in the sense of Dasein's passive mode of *being-in-the-world*; above all as the disposition, or the affectedness [*die Befindlichkeit*][109] and 'thrownness' [*die Geworfenheit*]. Parallell to these we have those existentials characterized by Dasein's active mode of *being-in-the-world*: understanding [*Verstehen*] and 'projection' [*Entwurf*].

By using the example of Dasein's character of 'care' [*Sorge*] (i.e., the existence characterized as already being in relation to others through the mode revealed as thrownness), this 'care' can show itself differently, due to the possibility of authentic and inauthentic self-understanding.

According to Heidegger, my self-understanding is the result of my practical understanding and handling of things, tools for example. We understand ourselves in terms of our activities.[110] Authentic self-understanding occurs in the moment [*Augenblick*] when we resolutely and at once [Entschlossenheit] grasp through repetition [wiederholen] those aspects of our past which are significant for the present situation. At the same time it points towards, or anticipates [vorlaufen], a new, possible future understanding of meaning through the projective character, as something for-the-sake-of-which. By always existing in the back-and-forth-manner of Dasein's temporality, we can point out the circularity of the hermeneutical situation in which we are always situated. We can also show how the existential character of Dasein's temporality [Zeitlichkeit] might result in authentic self-understanding, by our grasping the existential, ontological structures of Dasein's 'being'.

Against this background we can approach the notion of 'existential phenomena'. According to Heidegger, the very acts that uncover *'being'* are phenomena. Thus, *being-in-the-world* is a phenomenon if and only if the Dasein, by asking the question of 'being', discloses its own 'being'. Accordingly, the relationships of 'being' can become phenomena if and only if the particular being of a specific relation is uncovered.

We have seen that *Dasein's being-in-the-world* also means an uncovering in the sense of the unveiling of a possible function of a familiar extant entity—a thing or an object—through its relationship to the Dasein, as *vorhanden* or *zuhanden*. The meaning of a particular thing, it was said above, must be uncovered before we can know how to use it. This revelation, this uncovering of meaning, also constitutes a phenomenon. But these are phenomena of the world[111] and should be distinguished from phenomena characterized by temporality, from existential phenomena.[112]

I am not personally convinced that 'care', 'death', 'guilt', 'fear', etc. are phenomena in their own right although we can easily get that impression when reading Heidegger's *History of the Concept of Time*, where most of the central notions

---

[109] The translation, 'affectedness', is suggested by H. Dreyfus to avoid a reading of the term as some kind of mental state or a behaviouristic use, indicating something belonging to the outer conditions. Cf. Dreyfus, 1991, p 168f.

[110] Okrent, 1988, p 36.

[111] Cf. Heidegger, 1982, p 168.

[112] Cf. Heidegger, 1982, pp 287–289.

are termed 'phenomena'. Following what has been said above, I propose that in our being with others we consider *care, death, guilt, fear,* etc. as phenomena only in situations where they point towards a renewed self-understanding in which our own 'being' is uncovered. For example, it is not possible for me to experience my own death now; maybe I will do all that is in my power to escape the understanding that I will die one day. If so, this is a behaviour that will force me into an inauthentic self-understanding. However, by experiencing the death of others I can direct myself towards an authentic self-understanding. Functioning in that way, *care, death, guilt, fear,* etc. are existential phenomena, since they uncover the authentic ways of our most genuine capacity for being-with others and for being ourselves.

Before discussing Gerardus van der Leeuw's view of the phenomenology of religion, I will sum up some of the central points of this chapter, which are important for the coming analyses:

1. According to Heidegger, phenomenology has to do with fundamental ontology. By choosing this focus he departs from Husserl, for whom phenomenology is first of all an epistemological effort.

2. The question of fundamental ontology is concerned with 'being', as the ground for everything that is. In Heidegger's phenomenology, the question of 'being' is the starting-point for human existence as being its foundation.

3. It is significant for us human beings that we can ask the question of 'being'.

4. Human existence [Ek-sistenz] is characterized as 'Dasein'.

5. As Daseins we are always *being-in-the-world*. This is Dasein's main characteristic described both as being-with and being-toward.

6. The world of the Dasein is not static. Heidegger makes a distinction between 'world' and 'nature'. Nature is all that exists independent of any present Dasein. The world is what Dasein recognizes, either as being-present or being-at-hand. The world is thus 'mind-dependent', while nature is 'mind-independent'.

7. As Daseins we always exist in time. For Heidegger the human being, dwelling in the world, is a project characterized by 'temporality'. He talks about the 'exstases of temporality', i.e., of the past, the present, and the future. As Dasein, I am always concerned with these three exstases when I try to cope with my existentiell situation. In terms of temporality, this means that in a present situation I must try to find ways to move ahead. This moving is not done arbitrarily, but with an expectation of the outcome, and the outcome of this expectation belongs to the future. At the same time, I can go back and compare my present situation with memories of previous experiences which belong to the past.

8. Dasein's main struggle is to find a way to exist that reveals its 'being' as it really is. This is revealed through the existentials, i.e., through the phenomena of 'being', such as the phenomena of 'guilt', 'awe', 'love', 'care', 'death', 'fear', etc.

9. These phenomena can become available to us through hermeneutics. We always have some idea about what lies ahead of us. While engaged in the hermeneutical process, I know something of what I am to interpret. Thus, the hermeneutical situation is a circle. The point of departure is my idea about what is to be interpreted. I can compare both the situation and the object to other situations and

objects already known. Thus I can find correspondences and discrepancies before I make my conclusions. That being done, I am in some aspect back on square one again but now in another sense, because I have reached new conclusions.

10. To be able to live my life in such a way that I am aware of 'being' as the foundation of my existence, I have to interpret my existentiell situation. I can do this by comparing my life-situations to those of other people, since 'being' is the same for all. The sameness, the sharing of human existence is existential. The ways in which other people have coped with their circumstances can be of guidance for my own efforts. I can become aware of these possibilities by learning from others. All this is possible because of Dasein's historicity, and it can become accessible to me through history when I compare my own situation with that of others. However, I must not copy another person but I must always act on my own although in the light of others. If I do not do so, I will cease to be myself, and will instead become a copy of the other person, *das Man*.

In the next chapter we will analyse how Gerardus van der Leeuw expounds Heidegger's ideas of the existential situation, and those of existential phenomena as they are revealed through religion. We shall also see how van der Leeuw relates his ideas of the phenomenological method to Heidegger's views of temporality, historicality, and hermeneutics as a method.

CHAPTER 4

Gerardus van der Leeuw's Construction of a Philosophical Phenomenology of Religion

In this chapter I will first of all analyse the model for the phenomenology of religion as presented by van der Leeuw in his *Phänomenologie der Religion*. The main question is centred around the use and understanding of phenomenology in general, when applied to religious studies, as the phenomenology of religion. It is in other words a question of whether phenomenologies of religion based on philosophical, existential phenomenology should be considered as (a) a way of life in general or, as (b) a scientific method. A combination might also be envisaged.

As will be shown below, there are several different opinions among scholars who have studied his work about the degree of philosophical influence and ambitions in van der Leeuw's phenomenology. As far as I can see, his phenomenology seems to be based on his understanding of religion:

> THAT which those sciences concerned with Religion regard as the ***Object*** of Religion is, for Religion itself, the active and primary Agent in the situation or, in this sense of the term, the ***Subject***. In other words, the religious man perceives that with which his religion deals as primal, as originative or causal; and only to reflective thought does this become the Object of the experience that is contemplated.[1]

Religion, and especially religious experience, is thus referred back to a subject, characterized as a primary agent. This agent can be identified as God. But, as van der Leeuw continues, our concept of God is not a definite concept. The case, he says, is often that our understanding of God does not completely coincide with the referent, that is, with the subject. This gives him reason to talk about religious experience as a relationship to a "***highly exceptional*** and ***extremely impressive*** *'Other'*"[2], or 'Somewhat'.

My reason for drawing attention to this point here is that I believe it to be important for (an appreciation of) van der Leeuw's discussion on the formation of a phenomenon. The question is what we experience when, following the phenomenological method, we re-experience religious experiences for the purpose of reconstructing their content.

Phenomenology of Religion as a Scientific Method for Investigating Religious Experiences

Before we can provide an analysis of the notion of the 'phenomenon' as used by van der Leeuw, an answer to the following questions must be determined:

---

[1] van der Leeuw, 1986, p 23.
[2] van der Leeuw, 1986, p 23.

Firstly, if it is possible to trace a clear influence from Husserl, can van der Leeuw then be said to make use of the same distinction as Husserl does between the phenomenon as appearance [Erscheinung] and as the thing that appears [Erscheinendes], and between the experience as an act and the content of the act, i.e., that which has been experienced? If so, this will have consequences for what is regarded as a religious phenomenon, whether it is the experience itself or the content of that experience. This will have consequences for determining to what phenomenology as a method should be applied. There is already an indication in the quotation on the first page of this chapter that, according to van der Leeuw, a reconstruction of previous experiences (our own and/or other people's) cannot in any sense of completeness give access to these experiences or to their content.

Secondly and if so, does van der Leeuw share Husserl's epistemological view that the investigation of phenomena is part of a search for certitude? This would guarantee a foundation for religion through the phenomenological investigation into religious experiences.

Is, thirdly, van der Leeuw's use of the notion of the phenomenon more closely related to the pragmatically oriented, ontological, and conceptual understanding of phenomena formulated by Heidegger than to the epistemological understanding formulated by Husserl? Does this understanding lead to a view which incorporates a hermeneutical understanding of the phenomenon? This would mean that phenomena should be considered as expressions of the human experiences which people have when coping with themselves and their surrounding world.

Finally, if scholars have overestimated the influence from philosophical phenomenology, especially with regard to the notion of the phenomenon, how should we then understand and legitimize the phenomenological method used and favoured by van der Leeuw? In other words, do we misunderstand van der Leeuw's intentions by putting a strong emphasis on philosophical phenomenology as the background against which the phenomenology of religion ought to be interpreted as Mircea Eliade and van der Leeuw do?

The first question concerns that which is more precisely referred to as 'the phenomenon'. If we use it in the Husserlian sense of appearance, it is ultimately isolated to the intentional act of an isolated subject, and as such it cannot be shared between two or more subjects. When used in the sense of the thing that appears, that is as memory content, we communicate whatever it is, and we have moved from the presuppositionless state of the phenomenological method towards reflection. Because as soon as we start reflecting on what has appeared, we relate this to our former experiences and knowledge, and in doing so we move away from the attitude where we approach the world free from prejudice. As seen in the quotation of van der Leeuw mentioned above, it is the already established understanding of religion that helps us move from presuppositionlessness toward reflection on religious experiences. Thus, the expression 'religious phenomenon' is problematic not only with regard to the demand for presuppositionlessness because of the reference to 'religious', but also because we already know what we are looking for, i.e., religious experience, and we are already coloured by ideas of what religion actually is.

The second question, whether the investigation of phenomena is part of a search for certitude, will be seen to raise further problems when we investigate the meaning of the phenomenology of religion—and the term 'phenomenon' is used in the Husserlian sense, as appearance, and not in the sense of the appearing thing [Erscheinendes] (the experienced).

The third question is also complex since it relates to at least two different aspects. The first can be said to refer first to Heidegger's use of the notion of the phenomenon as *"that which shows itself in itself"*,[3] and then to the human situation as being-in-the-world. As we saw, Heidegger maintained the idea that the world is that which Dasein recognizes as its dwelling-place. It consists of other Daseins and recognized objects that have become intra-worldly through their occurrence and availability. Heidegger's idea of transcendence in its epistemological sense also minimizes the possibilities to consider manifestations of something extra-worldly through things, through entities. Even though God has being, God does not have existence[4] which can be understood, because there are no manifestations of God.

> Least of all can the Being of entities ever be anything such that 'behind it' stands something else 'which does not appear'. 'Behind' the phenomena of phenomenology there is essentially nothing else; on the other hand, what is to become a phenomenon can be hidden.[5]

Our fourth problem to be solved is more concerned with labelling the method of investigation as *phenomenology*. If the analysis would show that, even though one talks about religious phenomena and one uses methodological principles from Husserlian phenomenology (including terms like 'epoché' and 'eidetic vision'), the epistemological claims of philosophical phenomenology and of the phenomenology of religion are incommensurable, is it then still justifiable to talk about 'phenomenology' when studying occurrences from the world of religion and religious life? This question is of course only relevant if the use of phenomenology is limited to its philosophical sense.

The Characterization of Religious Phenomena

According to van der Leeuw, the phenomenon as appearance has an intentional character. The manifestation of a phenomenon as appearance concerns both what appears and the person to whom it appears.[6] The phenomenon is a something; this something shows itself, or appears. And just because it appears it is a phenomenon.[7] This circular description does not provide us with much clarity on van der Leeuw's understanding of the word 'phenomenon'. It is rather a description of his idea of the intentional character of an appearance, i.e., of a phenomenon.

---

[3] Heidegger, 1993b, p 51.
[4] Valen-Sendstad, 1969, p 78.
[5] Heidegger, 1993b, p 60.
[6] van der Leeuw, 1986, p 671, 1956, p 768.
[7] van der Leeuw, 1986, p 671, 1956, p 768.

Because of the intentional character of the phenomenon, in the sense that the 'something' requires a 'someone' to whom it appears, the phenomenon is, according to van der Leeuw, neither a pure object nor, as he states, the 'Object'. The 'Object' is, as pointed out above, simultaneously the 'Subject'[8] in the sense of the active agent—God. Thus van der Leeuw concludes that the 'Object' should not be dealt with in the field of phenomenology but rather in that of metaphysics.[9] However, the phenomenon is not something purely subjective, something limited to the consciousness of the person who perceives the appearance. Rather, the phenomenon is "... an object related to a subject, and a subject related to an object ...".[10] If this is to be comprehensible, we have to distinguish between the various object-subject relations used by van der Leeuw.

There is first of all the religious subject-object understanding, in which the object of religion is in fact the 'Subject', i.e., God, or the not fully revealed primary agent manifested as a 'somewhat', as the not fully immanent 'Other'. Then, van der Leeuw introduces yet another subject-object relation concerning the phenomenon, the manifestation of this 'Other', observed by someone in its appearance. The problem is that we are dealing with two subjects. On the one hand there is the subject, i.e., the person who observes the appearance. On the other hand there is the subject of religion, i.e., the primary agent, God, acting as a 'something' becoming manifest in the appearance. These two aspects must not be conflated in the analysis of van der Leeuw's notion of phenomenon.[11]

The reference back to a primary acting agent, being the subject of religion, will also be important when it comes to the question of whether van der Leeuw makes theology the starting-point of his phenomenology of religion, as stated by J. Waardenburg,[12] or if this is to be regarded as an independent discipline. The latter seems to be van der Leeuw's own intention. He makes a clear distinction between the phenomenology of religion and theology in *Phänomenologie der Religion*. The reason is that he wants to avoid the risk of being normative as well as the risk of metaphysical speculation.[13] According to van der Leeuw, these fallacies characterize theology as well as philosophy: "... phenomenology of religion is not theology. For theology shares with philosophy the claim to search for truth, while

[8] Cf. van der Leeuw, 1986, p 461, 1956, p 525.
[9] van der Leeuw, 1986, p 671, 1956, p 768. In the second edition of *Phänomenologie der Religion* (1956) the Object as the actual reality is described as "die wahre Wirklichkeit, deren Wesen von der Erscheinungen Schein nur verdeckt wird".
[10] van der Leeuw, 1986, p 671. Cf. 1956 p 768. In German: "... *das Phänomen ist ein subjektbezogenes Objekt und ein objektbezogenes Subjekt.*"
[11] As we later on will see, we can here find crucial evidence of van der Leeuw's transformation of the Husserlian and Heideggerian notions of the phenomenon. If we in Husserl conceive of the intentional relation as an internal relation, i.e., the intentional object only exists as such in my consciousness regardless of whether the actual object exists in reality or not. In relation to Heidegger it is not a question of a transcendent being acting and becoming manifest. It is being as such that is understood in terms of 'availableness' or 'ocurrentness'. van der Leeuw can be said to defend a form of mind-dependency at the same time as he accepts the existence of God whether human beings know of it or not.
[12] Waardenburg, 1978, p 223.
[13] van der Leeuw calls the speculation about the nature and being of God "a specific metaphysics". Cf. van der Leeuw, 1986, p 671.

phenomenology, in this respect, exercises the intellectual suspense of the *epoche*".[14]

This idea that both theology and philosophy claim to be searching for truth must be seen against a situation in which theology is studied at confessional institutions, thus being an instrument for the confession itself where 'truth' can be replaced by 'God'. Philosophy's search for truth means something different. It can mean the search for some ultimate foundation on which our ideas are founded or it can mean that our arguments can be scrutinized and verified on the basis of philosophical premises. Waardenburg states that van der Leeuw's phenomenology of religion arises out of theology. This does not contradict van der Leeuw's own distinction, which supposes that the phenomenology of religion is not identical with theology. Religious experience is, of course, in one way or another, always connected to the beliefs that theology expounds, but that phenomenology does not approach these experiences in a theological manner.[15] Although the relationship between theology and the phenomenology of religion seems to have been clarified, the idea of a subject acting behind the appearance still indicates that, in the case of van der Leeuw, there is some intimacy between theology and the phenomenology of religion.

It seems possible to relate van der Leeuw's writings on the phenomenon as appearance to Husserl's basic idea of the phenomenon. But, if one takes van der Leeuw's understanding of religion as the point of departure, Husserl's fundamental idea of the presuppositionlessness will be problematic. Taking van der Leeuw's understanding of religion as the starting-point, it implies certain presuppositions which will create an idea of what is supposed to be the object of the phenomenological investigation. van der Leeuw already has certain ideas about God, about religion and about what religious experiences are all about. These presuppositions are not, as far as I can see, bracketed by van der Leeuw. This means that Husserl's request for presuppositionlessness will not be wholly observed by van der Leeuw. As we saw, Husserl's idea of presuppositionlessness is aimed at liberating myself in the act of experiencing something from all surrounding knowledge and attitudes that might distract my seeing, by colouring my idea about what I have in front of me. It also requires a bracketing of the 'know-how' and 'know-what' of the sciences. Husserl regarded them as not completely trustworthy, because at times, when compared or matched, they would contradict each other, due to their different systems of explanations and truths. This is the reason why Husserl called them 'regional ontologies'.

According to Husserl, presuppositionlessness is not established unless we free ourselves wholly from an epistemic relation to science. We must therefore ask ourselves whether it is enough to follow van der Leeuw in talking about the 'Subject' of religion, without defining it as 'God' but by calling it 'the Other', 'the Somewhat' etc. This terminology still seems to belong to theology and to the language of religious interpretations.

---

[14] van der Leeuw, 1986, p 687.

[15] See George A. James in his article "Phenomenology and the study of religion: The archaeology of an approach". James, G.A, 1985, p 333f., n62.

These arguments, claiming that van der Leeuw does not follow Husserl's idea of presuppositionlessness, seem adequate when we take into consideration that which would concern the scholarly study of religious experience. An objection may be that this reading does not focus on that which van der Leeuw aims at illustrating, namely, that the very act during which a person experiences something is not in itself coloured by any presuppositions. However, the reflection of what occurred or happened during the appearance or our reflections on what has been said to have happened etc. can be coloured by presuppositions.

This objection is important because there is, as far as I can see, a clear tension between the idea of the phenomenon as appearance (where the intentional object is not defined in terms of epistemological content) and the phenomenon as that which appears (which emphasizes the phenomenon as the content of the experience rather than as the experience itself). But, if we continue to relate van der Leeuw's notion of the phenomenon to the one of Husserl, there is also the problem with the actual empirical reality of the intentional object.

Husserl suggests, as we saw above, two possibilities. He distinguishes between intentional acts, where the reference exists as extant objects, and intentional acts, where the intention (the reference to an object) exists but not the object itself. The former refers to the notion of experiences of intentional existence and the latter to experiences of intentional inexistence. As was pointed out earlier, all representations of gods, angels, etc. should, according to Husserl, be referred to as 'intentional experiences of intentional inexistence'. However, this does not mean that the intentional object is not present. It is always present as at least a mental object in the consciousness of the experiencing subject. Thus, there are differences between intentional acts where (a) the intentum is given as an object existing outside/extra-mentally vs the subject, and (b) where the intentum is a re-presentation as an object which does not necessarily exist extra-mentally.

The problem that I find the most challenging is thus not the presence of the object in the mind of the subject, but how we express the presence. The intentional object is present whether or not we talk about intentional acts as presentations or re-presentations, but there is still a difference between what Husserl terms 'fulfilled' and 'unfulfilled' intentions.[16] I understand Husserl's term 'fulfilled' as the correspondence between the intention and the intentum. Being 'fulfilled' should thus mean a complete coverage of the various aspects of the intentum by the intention. According to my previous analysis of Husserl's thinking, the essence of an object is not completely grasped in one single act of perception. To be able to grasp the utmost of the essence, we must return to the object of the intentum and add or exclude further attributes, until we can perceive it in its essence. The degree of fulfillment of an intention can thus vary but this seems only to apply to intentional acts, where the objects are genuine presentations, i.e., where there is a correspondence between the object of the intentum and the external existence of the object.

I will illustrate what I have tried to indicate above. In this passage van der

---

[16] Cf. Hopkins, 1993, § 16, p 35f.

Leeuw discusses things as bearers of 'power', that is bearers of the 'Wholly Other':

> To the primitive mind, ... the thing is the bearer of a power; it can effect something, it has its own life which reveals itself, and once again wholly practically. During an important expedition, for example, an African negro steps on a stone and cries out: 'Ha! are you there?'[17]

When thinking in terms of the phenomenon as appearance and leaving the question of presuppositionlessness aside, does the example then illustrate an intentional act in the sense of a sensation, a presentation, or as a phantasm, a representation? Since the point of the matter is not the stone as such but its potential as a bearer of power, I would guess that Husserl would characterize it (if he were ever interested in the matter) as a phantasm. This does, however, not mean that the intentional object, the 'you' in the example, is not given in the mind of the subject (of the African). I would also interpret it as an illustration of an intentional act, where the object of the intentum (the 'you') is of intentional inexistence (it does not necessarily exist in palpable selfhood). This would also mean that the intention is empty:

> On the one hand, unfulfilled significative intentions are characterized by Husserl as 'empty', since the intentional object toward which the intentional regard is directed does not manifest itself qua its 'palpable selfhood'.[18]

It is not relevant to van der Leeuw's thinking whether the intentional act is one of 'intentional inexistence' or not. His point is only that someone has this experience of the something that sticks out as wholly other than the ordinary. Yet, I think it is possible to talk about an experience, a phenomenon in this case, and that both Husserl and van der Leeuw would agree, although for different reasons. Husserl would regard it as an experience of intentional inexistence, since we cannot guarantee the external existence of the object. van der Leeuw would not characterize it as an experience of intentional inexistence because of his basic understanding of God as existing but to whom we do not have full access; thus the object exists as an external reality.

Another question must now be raised. It will concern the relation between a phenomenon proper, where something appears to someone in an actual ongoing experience (lived experience), and the possibility for another person to re-experience the same phenomenon in the same actuality, and the ability to talk about it as a phenomenon in the same sense. At this stage of my analysis I would claim that the phenomenon defined as appearance (that which shows itself) is, according to Husserl and Heidegger, bound to an experiencing subject. In the sense of appearance used by Husserl it is attached to a subject, and in its temporal aspect it is

---

[17] van der Leeuw, 1986, p 37. The term 'primitive' is not used by van der Leeuw as an evolutionary term, but rather indicates an archaic state of mind unaffected by western cultures and especially the western scientific attitude to the world.

[18] Hopkins, 1993, p 36. Cf. Levinas, 1985, on Husserl's 'form of representation' and the relation between the 'representative' and the 'matter', p 72f.

limited to the 'now-phase'. Thus it is a primary phenomenon. As a phenomenon in the past, it belongs to the subject's memory and there the appeared thing exists as contents of consciousness; as such it is a secondary phenomenon. As conscious content, the phenomenon can be communicated as part of the subject's stored memory and knowledge. However, as an outside observer, a phenomenologist of religion has no access to primary phenomena other than their own. What seems to be regarded as 'phenomena' in the phenomenology of religion are both primary and especially secondary phenomena. Secondary phenomena can be transformed, handed over, and manifested in myths and through rites etc.

It seems to me as if van der Leeuw sometimes regards all sorts of accounts of experiences, and especially of religious ones, as phenomena without observing the distinction made by Husserl between the experience and the experienced. That is at least the impression given by the reading of the first part of the following quotation as an account of the experience and the second part as an account of the experienced:

> As phenomenologists, therefore, we must regard as valid revelation whatever presents itself as such. ... The phenomenologist can only discuss what is reported to him; he can listen for the authentic sounds and describe the objects wherein, according to the believer's own statements, revelation has for him been effected.[19]

Although van der Leeuw uses the term 'phenomenon', he nevertheless shows hesitation. He begins the chapter on "The Phenomenology of Religion" with the following observation:

> PHENOMENOLOGY is the systematic discussion of what appears. Religion, however, is an ultimate experience that evades our observation, a revelation which in its very essence is, and remains, concealed. But how shall I deal with what is thus ever elusive and hidden? How can I pursue phenomenology when there is no phenomenon?[20]

This is fully coherent with Heidegger's idea that there is nothing behind the phenomenon.[21] According to van der Leeuw's understanding the active agent, 'the Subject', never reveals itself completely. Thus manifestation of 'the Subject' cannot be considered as a phenomenon in the sense of a complete appearence of essence. He is talking about a phenomenology of religion, and since phenomenology seeks the phenomenon,[22] a religious phenomenon must exist. For the purpose of identifying more clearly what van der Leeuw has in mind when talking about religious phenomena, we have to turn to his description of the phenomenological procedure. It starts with assigning names and making categories. He gives examples of sacrifice, prayer, saviour, myth, etc., and makes the following remark

[19] van der Leeuw, 1986, p 566.
[20] van der Leeuw, 1986, p 683.
[21] When discussing van der Leeuw's view of phenomenology and his use of epochē, we will be constantly reminded of the similarity between Heidegger's and van der Leeuw's ways of formulating the matter of the integrity of the phenomenon, that is, that there is nothing behind it.
[22] van der Leeuw, 1986, p 671.

about the procedure: "In this way it appeals to appearances".[23] In other words, phenomenology has nothing directly to do with the original appearances, i.e., with the original phenomenon as appearance [Erscheinung].

This lack of clarity takes us back to the Husserlian distinction between the appearance itself and the appearing thing. I am not prepared to declare this distinction as the solution to this particular problem, but see it rather as an opening. I want us to move on instead to van der Leeuw's conception of phenomenology, and in particular to his conception of the phenomenology of religion, where we may be able to find further details about his view of the phenomenon.

The *Epilegomena* does not clarify what van der Leeuw finds most important to investigate. His phenomenology of religion is directed towards experiences, i.e., towards phenomena experienced by other people and not by the investigating students and scholars of religion. In that sense his phenomenology is different from Husserl's because van der Leeuw moves from phenomenology towards the hermeneutics of life following Dilthey and Heidegger.

How then can we proceed to clarify the distinction between phenomena in the sense of that which shows itself, and phenomena in the sense of varieties of occurrences within a particular religious tradition, or between religious traditions characterized by N. Smart as expressions of the religious dimensions?[24] For this purpose I suggest that we can continue to make fruitful use of Husserl's distinction between phenomena as [Erscheinung] and [Erscheinendes], and I propose the following terminology: 'proper phenomena' are those which describe appearance and experience, and 'secondary phenomena' are those which refer to the appearing thing in the sense of the experienced, i.e., to the established, conscious content of the 'proper phenomena'. In the case of the phenomenology of religion I will make a corresponding distinction between 'proper religious phenomena', and 'secondary religious phenomena'. To be able to talk about secondary religious phenomena, we must bear in mind that these are normally based on proper religious phenomena.

The point is that while the phenomenon in the proper sense is temporal (that is, immediate to the intentional act and only then perceivable by the perceiving person), the secondary phenomenon can be communicated as the memory of a past experience of a proper phenomenon. Understanding phenomena in this sense makes it possible to see that van der Leeuw uses the notion in both senses, but the study of phenomena is related to phenomena in the sense of secondary religious phenomena. His use of phenomenology is therefore different from that of Husserl who refers basically to proper phenomena.

Whenever we approach an already established religious concept, be it a rite, a myth, or something else, we do not approach an experience which leads to a phenomenon in the proper sense. This process is already past, whether the time span is great or only the twinkle of an eye. The direct experience is not available to study. We only have access to remembrances of various experiences.

---

[23] van der Leeuw, 1986, p 688.
[24] Smart, 1989, pp 9–24.

van der Leeuw states that phenomenology arises from the fact that somebody discusses what has appeared, i.e., the phenomenon.[25] This could mean that phenomenology is restricted to a personal, subjective discussion about appearances. It could also mean that phenomenology of religion is an attempt to interpret these sorts of discussions which account for experiences. As such, this phenomenology will have very little to do with the phenomenologies discussed above. van der Leeuw, departing from both Husserl and Heidegger, holds that the phenomenon in relation to the person to whom it appears has three levels of phenomenality: relative concealment, gradual revelation, and relative transparency. These three levels correspond to three levels of life: experience, understanding, and testimony. The phenomenological procedure is constituted by the systematic or scientific employment of the attitudes of understanding and testimony.[26] van der Leeuw thus understands phenomenology as a clarification of what has appeared.[27]

Phenomenology and the Phenomenology of Religion

van der Leeuw does not primarily identify phenomenology as a science, nor its method as an opportunity for each of us to acquire epistemological certainty about the conscious content, founded on the relation between the individual subject and its immediate and direct perception of an external object belonging to the surrounding world. Both Husserl's phenomenology and Heidegger's philosophy of life (coloured by the former and formulated in reaction to it) are about our immediate relation to surrounding reality. This understanding of phenomenology, however, seems to be of only secondary importance to van der Leeuw.

Let us try to elaborate this a little further. van der Leeuw's usage of the notion of a phenomenon follows the tradition of defining a phenomenon as that which shows itself. Here he does not depart from Husserl and Heidegger. As we have seen, van der Leeuw uses this definition primarily in relation to the object of religion and to our confrontation with it:

> ... this Object is a departure from all that is usual and familiar; and this again is the consequence of the **Power** it generates. ... To this Power, in conclusion, man's reaction is amazement (*Scheu*), and in extreme cases fear.[28]

According to van der Leeuw, phenomenology arises when somebody begins to talk about an appearence experienced by them.[29] Our response to this sudden impact of something experienced as wholly other—the numinous experience, if we go along with R. Otto—is to communicate to others what has appeared.

Can this idea of the phenomenon and phenomenology be said still to be in line with Husserl and Heidegger? Disregarding for a moment the role of a transcendent active agent, I think that we can answer the question positively, at least in

[25] van der Leeuw, 1986, p 671.
[26] van der Leeuw, 1986, p 671.
[27] van der Leeuw, 1986, p 674.
[28] van der Leeuw, 1986, p 23, 28.
[29] van der Leeuw, 1986, p 671, 681.

principle. The reason is that van der Leeuw actually sees this transcendent agent as an integral part of reality, that is to say human reality. On this point he moves further than both Husserl and Heidegger do.

Herbert Spiegelberg characterizes van der Leeuw's phenomenology as an 'extra-philosophical phenomenology', and he sees van der Leeuw's specific contribution in the attempt to "link up an impressive array of the main types of religious phenomena with philosophical phenomenology".[30] Others, like Ingvild Sælid Gilhus, characterize van der Leeuw's phenomenology of religion as a 'hermeneutic phenomenology of religion', distinct from a 'typological phenomenology of religion'.[31] 'Hermeneutic phenomenology' stresses the description of the essence of the phenomenon and not external characteristics. 'Typological phenomenology' consists of a systematic study of religion which stresses religious concepts, myths and rites which are "classified and systematized from a comparative point of view".[32]

What kind, or type, of phenomenology is expounded in the postscript "Epilegomena" by van der Leeuw? Is it 'hermeneutical', as proposed by Ingvild Sælid Gilhus, or is it 'extra-philosophical', although coloured by insights in philosophical and psychological phenomenologies, as proposed by Herbert Spiegelberg, or is it almost without any connections to philosophy at all, as proposed by Jacques Waardenburg,[33] or is it in debt to the phenomenology of Husserl, as proposed by Bleeker? In *The Sacred Bridge*, Bleeker clearly suggests an influence from Husserl on van der Leeuw. This influence must be taken into consideration when attempting to understand the latter's phenomenology:

> Nobody can fully understand the trend of a phenomenology of religion, as e.g. that of Van der Leeuw, if he does not realize how strongly the Husserlian principles have influenced this scholar.[34]

In an article in *Numen*, 1971, Bleeker holds on to this view:

> ... one should keep in mind that several students of phenomenology of religion have been influenced by the philosophical phenomenology of which E. Husserl is the chief exponent, or that they at least have borrowed their ideological apparatus from that branch of philosophy. ... I should only like to stress that in my opinion it is important to avoid the philosophical implications of the specific Husserlian method. My famous compatriot Dr G. van der Leeuw obviously has gone too far in this respect, as appears from the 'Epilegomena' of his wellknown 'Phenomenology of Religion'.[35]

Bleeker finds that, even though van der Leeuw's use of phenomenology may be philosophically correct, it might well create confusion when applied within the field of the history of religions. He also mentions especially the Husserlian princi-

[30] Spiegelberg, 1984, p 10.
[31] Sælid Gilhus, 1984, p 26f.
[32] Sælid Gilhus, 1984, p 28.
[33] Waardenburg, 1991a, p 32.
[34] Bleeker, 1963, p 3.
[35] Bleeker, 1971, p 15. Cf. Bleeker, 1963, p 3. The 1971 article is only slightly changed from the passage in *The Sacred Bridge*.

ples in use: the *epochē* and the *eidetic vision*.[36] The view both that van der Leeuw was influenced by the thinkers of the phenomenological movement of the first three decades of this century, and that he transformed and directed a more or less philosophical phenomenology towards the study of religious phenomena, is also supported by scholars like E. Sharpe, T. Ryba, and Å. Hultkrantz.[37] At the same time it must be said that van der Leeuw himself is reluctant to regard the relation between his understanding and his use of phenomenology and the phenomenology of Husserl. On the one hand, van der Leeuw is aware of terminological confusion in his earliest work on the phenomenology of religion. There is a danger of participating and contributing to this confusion when subsequent scholars work within the field of phenomenology without being aware of this confusion. van der Leeuw also indicates that his application is less of an epistemological nature (like that of Husserl), and more psychological.[38] Even so it is clear that van der Leeuw takes over Husserl's conception of the epochē in the sense of 'bracketing'.[39] This is such an important part of Husserl's phenomenology that it can hardly be neglected. When John Richard Plantinga simply concludes that: "While he borrowed the term *epoche* from Husserl, other than this van der Leeuw's debt to Husserl is virtually non-existent. He never wrote anything about Husserl ...".[40]

I think there is a risk of underestimating the role of the epochē in Husserl's phenomenology, and consequently of missing to see how this is closely connected to his theory of the phenomenon as well as to his theory of essences. One must, of course, also keep in mind that it is not only via a direct influence that Husserlian phenomenology is possible. As we shall see, the influence from Heidegger and Jaspers are in their turn based on, and reacting against, Husserlian phenomenological principles.

As was said earlier, van der Leeuw designed the task of determining labels as the first step of the phenomenological procedure. The examples of names: sacrifice, prayer, myth, etc., indicate that he follows the tradition of the phenomenology of religion introduced by Chantepie de la Saussaye. The latter used the term 'phenomenology' to characterize his systematization of religious data in his *Lehrbuch der Religionsgeschichte*.[41] There is an obvious similarity between van der Leeuw's and Chantepie de la Saussaye's ways of approaching the field of religious data and the order of systematization and presentation. An interesting part of this is the role of Hegel's phenomenology which both of them make references

---

[36] Bleeker, 1971, p 15f. Cf. Bleeker, 1963, p 3.

[37] Sharpe, 1975, p 224, 230, Ryba, 1991, p 231f, Hultkrantz, 1973, p 78f.

[38] van der Leeuw, 1925, p 4, n1, p 7, n1. In his editorial foreword to the book, Friedrich Heiler also underlines that phenomenology should not be understood in relation to the work of Husserl and Scheler, but rather in line of Tiele, Chantepie de la Saussaye and Lehmann. See "Vorwort des Herausgebers", footnote 1.

[39] van der Leeuw, 1935, p 68f.

[40] Plantinga, J. R., 1990, p 256.

[41] It is only in the first edition of the work from 1887 that he characterizes his science phenomenology of religion. In later editions, like the one from 1905, Chantepie da la Saussaye characterizes the method of combining and grouping different religious appearances as religious phenomenology [die religiöse Phänomenologie] which he regards as a bridge between the science of religion and the philosophy of religion. Cf. Chantepie de la Saussaye, 1905, p 5.

to, because of Hegel's identification of the various modes for studying religion, and of identifying the harmony between idea and religious realisation, i.e., between the essence and the manifestation of religion.[42]

In tracing the philosophical roots of van der Leeuw's phenomenology of religion, both George James and Thomas Ryba compare the phenomenologies and notions of the 'phenomenon' of, among others, Lambert, Kant, Robison, and Hegel. In his analysis of the philosophical phenomenologies, Ryba concludes by defining phenomena and the task of the phenomenological method:

> A phenomenon is not a thing-in-itself ... Phenomena are the complex products of (1) a priori conditions of consciousness, (2) attentional, mnemonic and imaginative alterations and (3) irreducable structural characteristics (phenomenological essences). Phenomenological method is directed primarily, to disclosing the latter.[43]

In his analysis of the phenomenologies of religion of Bleeker and van der Leeuw, Ryba finds that they are influenced by the Husserlian notions of phenomenological and eidetic reduction. This influence is clearly indicated by the terms in use: 'eidetic vision' and epochē.[44] In the case of van der Leeuw, though, he makes the observation that:

> The Husserlian technique would be of similar value to Van der Leeuw's method, as well, for though Van der Leeuw conceives of the phenomenological technique correctly, at least according to its general outline, his explanations of the various constituent steps are vague.[45]

The vagueness of van der Leeuw's phenomenological technique has to do with seven stages identified by him. They are separated from each other only in a logical sense and not chronologically, since they occur simultaneously in the actual process. The stages[46] are as follows. (1) The assigning of names. This is, as van der Leeuw says, what speech first of all consists of. (2) Interpolation of the phenomenon into one's own life. The notion used for this process in the phenenological movement is normally *empathy*, though van der Leeuw prefers not to use it and warns the reader against reading too much of a feeling-aspect into the meaning. (3) Application of the epochē, that is restriction of empirical or metaphysical judgements regarding the truth or reality of the phenomenon. In the passage treating this stage, van der Leeuw makes the interesting remark which we have already noted: "Phenomenology is concerned only with 'phenomena', that is with 'appearance'; for it, there is nothing whatever 'behind' the phenomenon".[47] (4) Characterization and sampling of the results into structures of ideal types, following the pattern of Eduard Spranger in his *Lebensformen*.[48] (5) Hermeneutics in the sense of a *Verstehen*-analysis of the content of the manifestation

[42] Waardenburg, 1973, p 106. Cf. James, G. A., 1985, p 331, Sharpe, 1975, p 221f.

[43] Ryba, 1991, p 216, 226, 230.

[44] Ryba, 1991, p 241. Cf. Bleeker, 1971, p 15f., Leeuw, 1986, p 645f., 675f., 683, 687.

[45] Ryba, 1991, p 241.

[46] For the following discussion regarding the stages, see van der Leeuw, 1986, pp 674–678. Cf. Waardenburg, 1978, p 231f.

[47] van der Leeuw, 1986, p 675.

[48] Spranger, 1925, p 4f., 114f.

expressed in the appearance. (6) Control and correction of what has been under-stood phenomenologically of the appearence by means of empirical research (ar-chaeology, philology). (7) The experience of understanding [Verstehen] resulting in a testimony of what has been manifested and understood.

van der Leeuw makes an important remark in his section on *understanding*, ((5) above), when he states that "science is hermeneutics".[49] The hermeneutics in question is mainly influenced by Dilthey and Heidegger, but also by L. Bins-wanger. This influence is important when we qualify his method in terms of 'hermeneutical phenomenology'. We will separate between a phenomenological and a hermeneutical method by trying to point out the specific objectives for the two methods respectively.

Phenomenology of Religion as the Hermeneutics of Life

Following this headline, I will move from the role of phenomenology in van der Leeuw's approach towards his use of hermeneutics. The reason is that while many analyses of van der Leeuw's phenomenology of religion observe his hermeneuti-cal ambitions, there is nevertheless too strong an emphasis on the phenomenolog-ical aspect of his theory. I would like to see whether it is possible to interpret van der Leeuw's approach to religious experiences and occurences using the image of a triptych.

The first frame depicts an understanding of the phenomenology of religion in the manner discussed above, i.e., one which is more closely related to Chantepie de la Saussaye's way of making phenomenology into a philosophy of the history of religions. The difficulty in understanding what van der Leeuw actually means by 'phenomena' and 'phenomenology' is basically caused by the fact that he in his usage of the terminology departs from Husserl's and Heidegger's phenomenologies.

The second frame of the triptych has a clear hermeneutical character. Its image is of a psychological nature influenced by Dilthey and Jaspers. It is within this frame that we will find van der Leeuw's theme of finding the way of life in a chaotic world. Here we will also find his arguments which many scholars inter-pret as a critique of culture, and the romantic idea of a primitive, archaic remnant within human beings: if carefully delivered, observed and interpreted in the light of experiences of still surviving, 'primitive' cultures, this remnant would place even the life of the modern westerner more in accordance with human nature.

The third frame of the triptych, to which we will return below, is again of a phenomenological nature. The difference between this frame and the first frame is that now van der Leeuw's understanding of phenomenology in relation to the scholar, i.e., to the phenomenologist, will be taken into account. I will try to show that here we have to do with phenomenology in a Husserlian-Heideggerian com-bination, which means phenomenology as an epistemological-ontological method for the individual subject to gain adequate knowledge about, and a means by which to encounter, reality.

---

[49] van der Leeuw, 1986, p 676. To van der Leeuw 'science' in this context means the human sciences. Cf. Waardenburg, 1978, p 200f.

Hermeneutics for Interpreting Religious Experience

I will here try to analyse how van der Leeuw uses the notion of epochē in a limited fashion when he discusses phenomenology as the method for studying religious experiences, acts, etc. The notion of epochē, 'bracketing', in the Husserlian sense points out the need for a complete, though temporarily limited, withdrawal of pre-understanding caused by sets of values, judgements and knowledge that we already have. The epochē is a necessary requirement for us when we are to perceive in general that which shows itself to us in its own unconditioned way. As far as I can see, van der Leeuw makes use of the epochē in the Husserlian sense, but there are problems when his usage of the notion is related to his idea of phenomenology. Waardenburg has observed this discrepancy, and he concludes:

> For van der Leeuw the *epochē* basically was not the first reduction of Husserl (which implies another epistemology) but the effort the scholar made to waive and free himself of current opinions and his own assumptions, and open the way to what may be called the meaning of a phenomenon.[50]

The issue raised by Waardenburg needs to be looked at in some detail. The question is whether there really is a completely different understanding between van der Leeuw and Husserl regarding the role and practice of 'epochē'. What is put in brackets is first of all that which Husserl calls the natural standpoint, relating to the natural world, but this does not mean that the epochē functions as a tabula rasa. The world is still present to us as a reality of which we are conscious. It is our convictions about the world that has been put in brackets.[51] As Haglund points out, what is left after the application of the epochē are the pure phenomena and their essences.[52] The crucial problem that Waardenburg puts forward is implicitly indicated by van der Leeuw himself, who seems to know beforehand what he is looking for, namely various expressions of individual personal encounters with the 'Other'. While Husserl formulates, and constantly revises, his phenomenology as a rigorous science with a universal claim, van der Leeuw uses phenomenology in a very different way. For him phenomenology can be regarded in two ways. The first one is a way of identifying, naming, religious experiences of individuals other than the scholars themselves. The second one is rather a romantic use of phenomenology as a term for the individual scholar's[53] selfunderstanding, i.e., salvation.[54]

The point I have tried to make by using the phrase 'epochē limited' is that while van der Leeuw regards the epochē as intellectual suspense, he cannot be said to observe Husserl's principle of presuppositionlessness in a strict sense, since it is obvious that he has some kind of theological/religious pre-understand-

---

[50] Waardenburg, 1991b, p 89f.

[51] Cf. Haglund, 1977, p 44, Kohak, 1978, p 28.

[52] Haglund, 1977, p 45.

[53] I use the term 'scholar' here because van der Leeuw seems to direct his thinking in such a direction although he talks about man in a more general sense as well.

[54] van der Leeuw, 1986, p 681, 684.

ing. Thus, his use of *epochē* is not strict in the sense of a complete suspension of values and judgement in relation to the analysis of religious phenomena. He regards the application of epochē as the necessary principle for the suspension of truth-claims.[55]

Experience in General

One way of interpreting the notion of experience in van der Leeuw's work is to regard experience as the sole reminiscence of a phenomenon, but the phenomenon in itself may also be an experience. If the distinction between experience and the experienced—i.e., what we referred to above as the proper phenomenon and the secondary phenomenon—is not observed, the risk of confusing the use of the notion of the phenomenon is obvious. One way of clarifying van der Leeuw's own idea is to analyse his use of the notion of experience, and to see where this fits into his phenomenology.

Following the line of thought in Schleiermacher's and Dilthey's hermeneutics, van der Leeuw connects the notion of experience to the one of 'life'.[56] 'Life' in this sense is not to be confused with biological or physical life, but should be understood in the light of Dilthey's use of the term as a reference to the whole sphere of human life, and to the life of humanity in its socio-cultural organisations and achievements.[57] Using the distinction between the natural sciences and the humanities, Dilthey defined the task for the latter as the understanding of human life. Thus 'understanding' will be the key term by which to define the task of humanities.[58] van der Leeuw relates to Dilthey, especially to the latter's view on hermeneutics as the method for analysing the process under which understanding of the 'psycho-historical life' is established.[59]

The notion of 'life' seems to be the key to van der Leeuw's understanding of 'experience', particularly to what he calls the 'primal experience'. This is the experience on which our other experiences are founded, and it is irrevocably linked to the actual time in which it takes place. The temporality of experience and of life can be illustrated by the image of a chain. Every individual experience is represented by a link, and the linking together with previous links until an ever-growing chain takes place at the moment of each experience. Each actual experience belongs to the present, but as soon as it has passed, or has been performed, it is irrevocably linked together with all experiences of the past.

Since Dilthey seems to be the main influence on van der Leeuw on this point, it may be worthwhile to quot his explanation on the relation between experience and time:

---

[55] van der Leeuw, 1986, p 687.
[56] van der Leeuw, 1986, p 671.
[57] Dilthey, 1962; H.P. Rickman's (ed) introduction to *The Historical World and the Methods of History*, p 64.
[58] Jeanrond, 1993, p 51f.
[59] Cf. Makkreel, 1992, p 214–215 .

The present is the filling of a moment of time with reality; this is experience, in contrast to the memory of it, or to the wishes, hopes, expectations and fears about something which may be experienced in the future.[60]

Dilthey goes on to link the future, the present, and the past into a relational continuity by which life is seen as something temporal. 'The future' will always become 'the present' and end up as 'the past'. This idea reminds us of similar thoughts of temporality in both Husserl's and Heidegger's philosophies. Human life has a temporal character, where past, present and future are always in progress.

Life is present all over the globe in innumerable particular lives, and is lived and relived by every individual. Being but an instant of time present, it eludes strict observation. But in retrospect and in its objective manifestations Life is better capable of being fully grasped and meaningfully interpreted than life according to our personal knowledge and in its countless forms today, and thus it reveals everywhere the same identical traits and common features.[61]

It is the idea of the 'now' being present in the past, that the present and the future will allow us to capture the now of an already past experience. This is the background of van der Leeuw's statement that there is no difference between an experience having taken place two thousand years ago, and one which passed just a second ago. They are equal in the sense that they are both past and they cannot be fully re-lived again as first-time experiences, or as primal experiences [Urerlebnis]. Although it is tempting to interpret Husserl's idea of temporality in the light of Heidegger's notion of 'historicity' and of Dilthey's understanding of the past, I am not convinced that this would be adequate. Husserl is only talking in terms of primary and secondary memory in relation to a particular subject's consciousness. Whereas the recollection of the past (memories) belongs to secondary memory, the immediate past—i.e., the sequence in which the actual now dies away and is succeeded by the next now—belongs to primary memory and is defined as 'retention'.[62] van der Leeuw seems to go further by indicating that by re-experiencing past experiences, particularly those of other people, I can bring these experiences into my own life and can understand and act accordingly. Even though this idea has certain similarities to Heidegger's idea of historicality, Heidegger would not go as far as this because of the risk that the re-experiencing person may become *das Man*.

According to Dilthey and Heidegger, human life with its universal character, exemplified through individuals and expressed as inter-subjectivity (the past experiences of other people) can be made available to anyone. However, nobody must simply copy the life-experiences of others. According to Heidegger this would mean giving up the self, neglecting my personal potentials and becoming a neuter—*das Man*. The idea of the accessibility to the experiences of others is primarily related to Dilthey's insight that we are able to understand any sort of

[60] Dilthey, 1962, p 98.
[61] Kluback and Weinbaum, 1957, p 21.
[62] Carr, 1991, p 21f. Cf. Husserl, 1970c, p 52f.; 1989, p 105f.; 1992, §§ 10, 11, 14, 15, 16.

life-expression by analogy with our own past, as singular individuals and/or as a collective body. It has been further elucidated by Heidegger's development of Dilthey's hermeneutics, and in particular by the use of Heidegger's notion of 'historicity'.[63]

Lived Experience [Erlebnis]

We have already come across the, in my opinion peculiar, notion of 'lived experience'. Hans-Georg Gadamer provides a useful explanation of the meanings and relations between the two German words 'erleben' and 'Erlebnis'. Recognizing 'Erlebnis' as a secondary formation of the verb 'erleben', Gadamer first gives the basic meaning of 'erleben' as "to be still alive when something happens. [This then suggests:] ... the immediacy with which something real is grasped".[64] This is something different from what one might persume to know, based on experiences not guaranteed by oneself. These unguaranteed experiences can be those taken over from other people, or based on hearsay, imagination, etc. On the other hand experience as [Erlebnis] implies someone's own experience.[65] Considering the content of experienced [das Erlebte], Gadamer defines a second meaning of 'Erlebnis', namely the permanent content of our consciousness, i.e., memory. Thus 'Erlebnis' holds the two meanings of (a) erleben (the immediacy with which something is grasped), and (b) das Erlebte (the content of the experienced in the sense of what has been discovered as the lasting result of an act).

Turning to Dilthey's idea of the word 'Erlebnis',[66] in the sense expounded in his hermeneutics, Gadamer shows us that the concept of the given is of importance for the formulation of the content of 'Erlebnis'. The given or data [Gegebenheiten] are presented through spiritual creations of the past, like art and history. According to Gadamer, Dilthey tries to grasp by his concept of experience "the special nature of the given in the human sciences".[67] The given as the primary data to be interpreted present themselves as bearers of meaning:

> That is what the concept of experience states: the structures of meaning we meet in the human sciences, ... can be traced back to ultimate units of what is given in consciousness, unities which themselves no longer contain anything alien, objective, or in need of interpretation. These units of experience are themselves units of meaning.[68]

In *Epilegomena* van der Leeuw seems to build up his notion of experience by references to the German word 'Er-leben'. The difference between the two German words for experience, 'Erfahrung' and 'Erlebnis' presents a problem. By connecting and limiting the concept of experience as an act [Erlebnis] in the sense of (a) above, it can be distinguished from experience as a content [Erfahrung].

[63] Cf. Jeanrond, 1993, on Dilthey, p 56, and Ruin, 1994, pp 112–114.
[64] Gadamer, 1993, p 61.
[65] Gadamer, 1993, p 61.
[66] Erlebnis as a real unit in consciousness, therefore the translation 'lived experience'. Cf. Makkreel, 1992, p 8f.
[67] Gadamer, 1993, p 65.
[68] Gadamer, 1993, p 65.

This would then mean that when I talk about my personal experience of something, this experience [Erfahrung] is my experience and not the one of the listener, of the reader. By means of understanding in the Diltheyian sense, this personal experience [Erfahrung] of a particular individual can be grasped, in terms of results of actions, and understood by others by means of intersubjectivity constructed around psycho-historical life—a condition which all humans have in common.

The Context of Life

According to van der Leeuw, 'life' is intimately bound together with experience. This 'life' is not biological life but, as related to lived experience, it is temporal. When van der Leeuw writes that his own life which he "experienced while writing the few lines of the preceding sentence, is just as remote from me as is the 'life' associated with the lines I wrote thirty years ago, ... I cannot call it back",[69] he is saying that the 'I' of the moment cannot be recaptured in its original sense. In the process of remembering, the 'I' of the past is objectified by the 'I' of the present. Thus my own past 'I' is just as much another as is an actual other person for me.[70] According to van der Leeuw, life is "never and nowhere 'given'"; it must be 'reconstructed'.[71] The reconstruction of experiences is initiated by what he calls the 'sketching of an outline of reality', and this outline is called a 'structure'. This structure cannot be analysed into its constituting particulars but has to be understood as a whole. "Structure is reality significantly organized."[72] According to Dilthey, by whom van der Leeuw was influenced, the lives of others must be reconstructed if their meaning is to be understood. It is, says van der Leeuw, through meaning that we have access to the reality of primal experience. In the act of understanding [Verstehen], the meaning experienced by the interpreter, and the meaning experienced in the primal experience (regardless of whether it is my own or someone else's), are united into an "irrevocable one".[73] This idea is built on Dilthey's notion of intersubjectivity and its foundation in psycho-historical life which is common to all humans regardless of their historic time and context. The common quality is one of life and spirit. This spirit is manifested in the results of actions, thoughts and sayings. The idea is that when we approach these manifestations by means of the hermeneutic method, we actually recreate the process ourselves. The understanding gained is one which we share with the other person, and thus we create one irrevocable whole of the reconstructed and primal experience.

Following Sœlid Gilhus' analysis we can assume that this significantly organized reality is our consciousness of ourselves and our surroundings, and the particulars refer to our stock of experience. The particulars, the experiences as such, are unavailable for analysis because, as soon as they are past, they are never and

---

[69] van der Leeuw, 1986, p 671f.
[70] van der Leeuw, 1986, p 672.
[71] van der Leeuw, 1986, p 672.
[72] van der Leeuw, 1986, p 672.
[73] van der Leeuw, 1986, p 673.

nowhere to be repeated in their original mode. The method for reconstructing consciousness follows a phenomenological procedure.[74] According to van der Leeuw it is the expression of a religious experience that is to be understood by means of the phenomenological method. What is first of all required is to enter into, i.e., devote oneself to, the object. "... the phenomenologist does not seek causal connections but rather attempts to penetrate to the stream of consciousness in which the object participates."[75]

In summary, the primal experience—the lived experience—should be seen as phenomena.

(1) I have reached this conclusion against the background of an analysis, especially in the light of van der Leeuw's statement that there is nothing behind the phenomenon itself, and in agreement with his claim that the experience in its primal aspect is never and nowhere attainable again.

(2) The object of the attempted understanding is the expression of the experience, which may be called the conscious-content. Waardenburg points out that for van der Leeuw there is no difference between the observation content which the ego has of itself and that of somebody else: "the 'contents' of consciousness being the same, it is only the 'act' of observation which makes the difference".[76]

(3) Another problem concerns the notion of 'structure'; van der Leeuw claims that the 'structure', "the sketching of an outline within the chaotic maze of so-called reality" is, on the one hand, a connection that is understood, and that can only be analysed as a whole and not as its parts.[77] On the other hand, the structure can be comprehended from its constituent parts organizing reality in its meaning-fullness. Nevertheless, the structure is not the parts.[78]

(4) Structure and meaning are connected insofar as what is gained from understanding is meaning; the meaning of the interpreter and the meaning of the primal experience—so that structure is always 'experienced structure'. According to Waardenburg, van der Leeuw's notion of experience always designates a structure. Within this structure things are understood in meaningful connections. The structure-designating experience, i.e., the 'constructing experience', is distinct from the primal experience which cannot be repeated.[79]

(5) The structure is the first momentum in the process of reconstruction, and by reconstructing one's own life or the life of another person it is possible to gain *meaning* through the act of re-experiencing.

(6) Against this background I find it relevant to claim that experience and structure are not interchangeable.

---

[74] Sœlid Gilhus, 1984, p 35.
[75] Plantinga, J.R., 1990, p 127f. Cf. van der Leeuw, 1986, p 672.
[76] Waardenburg, 1972, p 164.
[77] In the chapter where Husserl's phenomenology was analysed we saw that he united the two relations, i.e., the primary relation and the mental relation into one connection which he called the phenomenological experience. The difference between Husserl's idea and the one of van der Leeuw is that for Husserl, but not for van der Leeuw, it is clear that both sides of the connection must be understood if the essence of the phenomenological experience is to be grasped.
[78] van der Leeuw, 1986, p 672.
[79] Waardenburg, 1972, p 165f., footnote 97.

(7) The understanding of meaning belongs to the '*Verstehen analysis*' in terms of reconstruction and re-experiencing according to Dilthey's '*hermeneutics of life*'. It is also important to underline that van der Leeuw's conception of understanding [Verstehen] is, at least in *Religion in Essence and Manifestation,* under strong influence of Spranger's ideas in *Lebensformen,* where understanding "... ein geistiges Formen ist"[80] and not an image or a construction.

(8) In my opinion, the notion of 'primal experience' should be interpreted in Husserlian terms of retention/primary memory. It belongs to the past and cannot be grasped in its original sense but only through reconstruction.

'Meaning' and 'understanding' are interrelated in van der Leeuw's work. Understanding gives meaning. Meaning results from a coherence between the understanding of the subject and the understandability of the object.[81] Understanding, which is the gateway to the meaning of the primal experience, gives the meaning of myself as well as of the reconstructed, re-experienced other. An individual experience of understanding in this sense is that which van der Leeuw calls an 'experiental unity' since it is founded on reconstruction through re-experience.[82] Meaning is a connection, a coherence between understanding and understandability, and it is against this background that van der Leeuw states that the understanding of a connection dawns on us as life-meaning.[83] In my interpretation, understanding should thus be regarded as a phenomenon. Recapturing what was said above on van der Leeuw's description of a phenomenon as a "subject related object and an object related subject", understanding as experience is a primal experience. The influence on the character of understanding [Verstehen] by Spranger, that is, Verstehen as "geistiges Formen" makes understanding—in van der Leeuw's phenomenology—religiously founded. This point is clearly stressed by Waardenburg and it is against this background that I am prepared to talk about a return to an existential, philosophical phenomenology as the third frame of the triptych:

> The act of *verstehen* is founded religiously, and the very reversal from 'understanding' to 'being understood', which is so characteristic for Van der Leeuw, may be seen as a dialectic between subject and object of *verstehen,* a dialectic which takes place in a religious dimension.[84]

Types and Ideal Types

We must interpret van der Leeuw's notions of the 'type' and the 'ideal type' against the background of the idea of achieving understanding [Verstehen] through re-experiencing previous experiences. Every individual, singular phenomenon taken

---

[80] Spranger, 1925, p 431f. : "... das Verstehen kein Abbilden, sondern ein geistiges Formen ist. Da es nun weder die volle Objektivität erreicht, noch seiner Natur nach in der bloßen Subjektivität verharren darf, so bleibt nicht übrig, als daß alles Verstehen seine Bedeutung darin hat, ein Drittes, Höheres, über dem Subjekt und dem Objekt zu erzeugen." Cf. van der Leeuw, 1956, p 770f., where he designates 'meaning' as a third realm existing 'above' mere subjectivity and objectivity. In so doing he makes reference to Spranger, 1925, p 436.
[81] van der Leeuw, 1986, p 672; cf. Waardenburg, 1972, p 170.
[82] Cf. Waardenburg, 1972, p 170.
[83] van der Leeuw, 1986, p 672f.
[84] Waardenburg, 1972, p 175.

as secondary phenomenon (i.e., as the lasting conscious content of an act of understanding) makes a 'type'. Thus the type is not identical with the phenomenon in its primary aspect, but rather it is to be regarded as an expression thereof. This interpretation also corresponds to Plantinga's interpretation, where he states that van der Leeuw's phenomenology is directed towards the expressions.[85]

Thus, types are examples of human experiences regardless of when (time) and where (culture) they take place. van der Leeuw can typify experiences in this manner by combining influence from the life-philosophy of Dilthey with Spranger's ideas of 'historicity' [Historisches Verstehen].[86] He also follows Heidegger's idea that understanding has a time-transcending character. At the same time van der Leeuw notes that, while there is no difference between my own ego's observation of itself and of another person's self-observing ego, understanding is, nevertheless, always subjective in the sense that reality is always the conceptualized reality of any experiencing individual.[87]

Waardenburg clarifies that, according to van der Leeuw, we have to distinguish between two different kinds of understanding: the static-phenomenological and the genetic-structural, in the process of understanding [Verstehen].[88] The static-phenomenological understanding visualizes the types as separate elements, as individual expressions of a phenomenon, and will thus consist of an unlimited number of individual expressions of phenomena, i.e., it is a stock of secondary phenomena. The second kind, the genetic-structural understanding, aims at distinguishing and structuring the various types according to their structural connections [verständliche Beziehungen],[89] i.e., according to the kind of context in which the individual experiences occur, and whereof the conscious content is an expression. The types are thus thematically structured which gives the notion of the 'ideal type'. As far as I can see, there is no clear distinction in van der Leeuw's own use between the 'type' and the 'ideal type' as he claims both to be "*perceptual* relationships, *structural connections*".[90] One way of clarifying the distinction between type and ideal type is to make use of the distinction between 'type' and 'token', which is made for the purpose of separating a category from one of its members. An individual (a token) is said to exemplify a type.[91] The choice of

---

[85] Plantinga, 1990, p 127, quoting van der Leeuw.

[86] Cf. Spranger, 1925, p 436.

[87] "*'Reality' is always **my** reality, history always **my** history, 'the retrogressive prolongation of man now living'*" as van der Leeuw writes in relation to empathy, the interpolation of phenomena in our own lives. van der Leeuw, 1986, p 674.

[88] Waardenburg, 1972, p 165.

[89] van der Leeuw takes over this terminology from Jaspers, and the latter claims that while being a part of history, the individual human being cannot experience history as something terminated, as a completed whole. To be able to reach an understanding of reality, we must observe it in its comprehensible realizations. As Jaspers writes: "*What seems merely individual as existence, however, turns for my knowledge into a general picture. In world orientation we see man as a historical quantity. ... what concerns us in any event is not his extraordinary effectiveness in reshaping existence, not even if we find him determining our own existence. Man is great only as a figure whose subjectivity and objectivity round themselves into a total, universal expression.*" Jaspers, 1970, p 353.

[90] van der Leeuw, 1986, p 673.

[91] See Kent Bach's article on the type-token distinction in the Cambridge Dictionary of Philosophy, 1995, pp 818–819.

'type' is due to the question of content; when it comes to the question of 'token', it depends on the individual frequency. When van der Leeuw speaks of 'types', 'ideal types', 'collective types' and 'individual personal types', these notions can be structured according to the type-token distinction as:

1) van der Leeuw's notions of 'type' and 'individual personal type' correspond to Peirce's notion of 'token', 2) van der Leeuw's notions of 'ideal type' and 'collective type' correspond to Peirce's notion of type.

As was said above the first step of the phenomenological procedure was to assign names to expressions, to what has been made manifest. Sharpe describes this step as the "assigning of names to groups of phenomena".[92] Examples of names were 'sacrifice', 'prayer', 'saviour', 'myth', etc. According to my interpretation these 'names' correspond to the notion of ideal types. For example: 'sacrifice' is an 'ideal type' while the particulars of the group of expressions, i.e., of the secondary phenomena, each correspond to a 'type'.

The Conception of Religion

In general, van der Leeuw approaches religion in two different ways. These two ways correspond to and determine the relation between phenomenology and theology. According to the first way, religion is conceived of as experience which is the concern of phenomenology. According to the second way, religion is conceived of as 'revelation' which is the domain of theology. Waardenburg clarifies this:

> (1) Religion can be observed as an intelligible experience, which is a human phenomenon and can be studied as such ... (2) Religion can be considered to be incomprehensible revelation, which revelation is not a phenomenon and cannot be studied; the essence of religion can only be grasped from God's point of view, and cannot be known. However, ... man's assertion about what has been revealed to him is a phenomenon and can be studied.[93]

Religion as experience follows the human struggle to come to terms with oneself and the surrounding world. Understood in this way, religion follows that which van der Leeuw calls the 'horizontal line', and religion as revelation is constituted by the "vertical way: from below upwards, and from above downwards".[94] According to van der Leeuw, if we follow the horizontal line in our search for ultimate understanding we are bound to reach the limit of our human efforts, and we can go no further. This limit is transcended when we find ourselves saved by God's grace.[95] This provides an understanding which means that one is being understood, as Waardenburg discussed above. As van der Leeuw writes: "... all understanding, irrespective of whatever object it refers to, is ultimately religious ... And that ultimately all understanding is 'becoming understood' ...".[96] All hu-

---

[92] Sharpe, 1975, p 234. Cf. van der Leeuw, 1986, p 674, 688.
[93] Waardenburg, 1972, p 173. Cf. van der Leeuw, 1986, p 679.
[94] van der Leeuw, 1986, p 680.
[95] Cf. Sharpe, 1975, p 233f., Waardenburg, 1978, p 232f.
[96] van der Leeuw, 1986, p 684.

man activities are destined for the purpose that our worldy struggles will ultimately reach the point where God will transcend into the world. Against this background we can interpret van der Leeuw's conviction that there is an "essential unity between religion and culture. Ultimately, all culture is religious; and, on the horizontal line, all religion is culture."[97]

In the light of van der Leeuw's last-mentioned insights, the transformation of the subject, the 'verstehen-experience' of finally understanding that one is understood, would also apply to the investigating subject, the phenomenologist. This might be regarded as a very romantic, idealistic idea. When seen in the light of his phenomenology of religion, it appears as a critique of modern culture. What we need is to "regard 'primitive' mentality as a general structure which embraces the same elements ... as our mentality (we possess several of them) but differently grouped".[98] We can also observe the background of van der Leeuw's opinion. As Hubbeling puts it, "by losing his original primitivity modern man had lost much of life".[99] It can only be restored by means of a phenomenological approach to experiences of reality.

Conclusions and Transition

Stated in the introduction of this thesis, my analysis of van der Leeuw's phenomenology of religion has been based on a profound wish to understand the relation between philosophical phenomenologies and this particular application of phenomenology to the study of religious phenomena. I have not been doing this with an intention of ascribing to van der Leeuw some philosophical ambitions which he may or may not have had. On that particular point I agree with Waardenburg and Plantinga. I am not primarily interested in explaining van der Leeuw's philosophical ambitions, but rather whether some ambition of my own could be clarified in the light of his understanding of the phenomenology of religion. My reason for choosing van der Leeuw is due to his effort to combine influences from philosophical as well as psychological applications of the phenomenology of his time with insights from the Science of the History of Religions.

In the light of the analysis above I am prepared to approach his phenomenology of religion through the image of a triptych. This image has been built around (1) a phenomenology of religion in the tradition of Chantepie de la Saussaye, (2) a hermeneutical analysis inspired by Dilthey, Spranger and Heidegger, and (3) a philosophical phenomenology which could be clarified with regard to epistemology if interpreted in terms of Husserlian phenomenology, and with regard to ontology, in terms of Heideggerian phenomenology. Much of the latter will be treated thoroughly in the next chapter. The whole of this three-fold image is surrounded by van der Leeuw's opinion that, following Hubbeling, religion is absolutely autonomous without the need for a foundation; religion is a given.[100]

---

[97] van der Leeuw, 1986, p 679, footnote 1.
[98] Plantinga, 1990, p 108, quoting van der Leeuw, 1928, *La structure de la mentalité primitive*, p 29.
[99] Hubbeling, 1987, p 70.
[100] Cf. Hubbeling, 1987, p 67.

Starting with the investigation of phenomena by means of a phenomenological method, we have seen that van der Leeuw makes use of some of Husserl's most central notions. These are 'epochē', 'eidetic vision', and 'empathy'.[101] It is also clear that the interpreters of van der Leeuw who claim a clear influence on his phenomenology from Husserl, build most of their arguments around these notions. They are right in doing so, but it is also important to ask in what respect we can say that van der Leeuw follows Husserl and when he departs, regardless of his terminological usage. I disagree with those who claim that there is only a slight influence from Husserl, and that this is restricted to the very terms in use, which have a completely different meaning when used by the two authors.

In the light of my analysis, I would like to make the following propositions: while referring to the phenomenon as that which appears, it is easy to slip into a philosophical view of the phenomenon following Husserl and Heidegger. This, however, is an obstacle. It can be said to be correct only if we limit ourselves to the notion as such, since van der Leeuw seems not to depart from the demand for presuppositionlessness. However, the all-embracing frame of our triptych is, as has been stated, based on van der Leeuw's conviction that all investigation of culture and religion is done within a religious domain. Nevertheless, I have tried to apply Husserl's distinction between primary phenomenon [Erscheinung] and secondary phenomenon [Erscheinendes] which, concerning phenomena as experience, corresponds to the distinction between 'primal-experience' (primary phenomenon) and the expression of an experience (secondary phenomenon). This helped me reach the conclusion that van der Leeuw's phenomenology of religion is, when dealing with religious phenomena, mainly an investigation of secondary phenomena. In doing so he follows the line of Chantepie de la Saussaye's view of phenomenology to a greater degree than those of Husserl and Heidegger. Husserl is concerned with the conditions under which we approach the world in a manner free from prejudice. This will strenghten our ability to become aware of the primary phenomena rather than confusing them with the secondary phenomena. Heidegger would see religion as one way of interpreting existential phenomena as a world view which goes beyond Heidegger's intentions. For him hermeneutics has to do with how to come to realize what existential phenomena are, and the role they play in our daily lives.

The second frame of the triptych concerns hermeneutics as the method for exposing the foundational structures of human existence, where interpretation will promote understanding of other people and of the self. I here depart from Sœlid Gilhus' description of van der Leeuw as a hermeneutical phenomenologist of religion. His hermeneutics comes closer to Dilthey's philosophy of life and to Heidegger's philosophy. The ideas about the temporal character of our lives together with the ideas about the temporality of experience expounded by these two philosophers, gave van der Leeuw the theoretical basis for concluding that there is no difference between one person's or another's experience of something particu-

---

[101] Hubbeling, though, is of the opinion that van der Leeuw is more influenced by Dilthey and Schleiermacher in his idea of empathy rather than by Husserl; cf. Hubbeling, 1987, p 70.

lar. The observation of one person's ego is no different from that of another person. The conscious content is the same, the difference is limited to the act. Thus we have the possibility by means of an empatic approach to re-experience the experiences of other people by reconstructing the context in which reality, through the coherence between the understanding subject and the understandability of the object, was grasped in its meaningfulness. This is an interpretative act, the result of which we can sort out in terms of various individual expressions of experiences (secondary phenomena) characterized as types. They also point out a wider, more universal, significance, i.e., to the 'ideal types' under which particular 'types' can be systematically organized.

The image of the third frame of the triptych is clearly related to the second one. Here I am more inclined to regard van der Leeuw's phenomenology as philosophical. My point is that van der Leeuw seems to mean that even the scholar cannot be a neutral subject. By following the procedures illustrated as image one and two above, we could say that in the last one the scholars themselves are moving towards the *verstehen-experience*. Through the course of re-experiencing and reconstructing experiences in the sense of secondary phenomena, van der Leeuw seems to indicate that this subject will also have experiences in the sense of primal experiences, and will thus experience that they are understood. The reason for calling this 'philosophical phenomenology' is that here we are actually facing ambitions that correspond to Husserl's idea of a 'presuppositionless' approach to the surrounding world by bracketing questions of truths and values, and of letting the appearances speak on their own accord. It also agrees with Heidegger's hermeneutical phenomenology where the concepts of 'historicity' and of Dasein's temporal character help us relate our life-situations to those of other people in our effort to choose ways of answering existential questions authentically.

CHAPTER 5

Phenomenology and the Acquisition of the World

So far, I have focused my investigation, in some detail, on how phenomenologists like Husserl and Heidegger from their perspectives try to approach the problem of human relations to the self and the world. From the Husserlian perspective, the central question was how to gain certitude beyond doubt in experiences. Husserl tried to find the answer to this by grasping the essence of the intentional object through the method of the phenomenological reduction. Heidegger, in his turn, seems to present us with an idea of two parallell modes of being. One is directed towards objects and things, i.e., towards extant entities, and to our possibility to understand them by means of their usefulness. This constitutes the pragmatic line. The other part of his thinking is directed towards human ways of existing. The understanding of human existence is a matter of clarifying the modes of being, in terms of fundamental relations. The crucial mode constitutes Being-in-the-World. The 'Da' of the 'Dasein' underlines the intentional character of being, expressed in terms of temporality, which makes up the foundation of the historical understanding of human nature.

The second part of my investigation dealt with the transmission of insights from philosophical phenomenology to the phenomenology of religion as envisaged by Gerardus van der Leeuw. A central problem is the interpretation of possible discrepancies between phenomenology as a general approach (the philosophical one) and phenomenology used for a much more limited purpose, i.e., for the study of religious experiences. I have tried to find a way of how to understand, from a non-phenomenological point of view, what is meant by a 'phenomenon'. By the term 'non-phenomenological' I want to indicate that I have tried to use an analytical language, as far as possible free from phenomenological terminology. My intention is not to claim that phenomenologists are reluctant to explain what they mean by certain notions or methodological considerations. I simply want to investigate whether we can express phenomenological ideas, in order to understand them, by another language and thus challenge a phenomenologist like Merleau-Ponty, who claims that: "Phenomenology is accessible only through a phenomenological method".[1]

I want to concentrate on a theme which may be considered trivial by many, namely the theme of how to conceptualize and acquire a world. This may seem trivial if we take for granted and consider as natural for human beings our capacity to relate to the surrounding world and to create images and world-views. From a philosophical point of view this is not the case. There are the fundamental philosophical problems which occur in the process of our relation to the surround-

---

[1] Merleau-Ponty, 1981, p viii.

ing world—problems of what exists, of the nature of being, of knowledge, of truth, etc. The crucial question in this investigation concerns the basis of the process in which the formulation of views of life takes place. What is at stake here is our understanding of ourselves and of the world.

The procedure I have in mind will take us from the phenomenologists' ideas of the world towards their ideas of intentionality and of inter-human relations in terms of inter-subjectivity. Against this background I will discuss, in the next and final chapter, a possible role for phenomenology within religious studies, which can provide a theoretical and methodological background for inter-disciplinary and inter-faith dialogue. This will be done by considering phenomenology as a model for identifying and expressing the meaning of life and for creating self-understanding. Thus phenomenology deals with the central components of both individual and collective views of life. It would help us to exchange perspectives on life and to provide the means for interactive interpretation among different opinions aiming at mutual understanding and respect.

I will continue to approach van der Leeuw's phenomenology from a philosophical perspective, fully aware of the alternative, which means regarding his phenomenology as non-philosophical. My reasons are simple. I cannot ignore the obvious similarities in terminology and methodological ideas between philosophical phenomenology and his approach, although I am aware of the argument that there is a difference of purpose between philosophical and religious phenomenologies. There is a problem here, as the acceptance of these differences could lead to an unwillingness to identify phenomenology of religion (i.e., that of van der Leeuw) with a philosophical phenomenology (i.e., that of Husserl). For example, if we approve of Husserl's phenomenological method, but not of its consequences (like the existence of objects with intentional inexistence) because some of our basic beliefs might be challenged, then we could just formulate another end for our use of phenomenology which would prove our point, anyhow. But the problem would still be there. I therefore want to discuss some of the problems which have arisen so far. The first one will concern the conceptual analysis of the notion of the world from phenomenological perspectives.

I will discuss the fruitfulness of distinguishing between 'world' and 'nature' (using Heidegger's distinction), between existing things and relations known through pragmatic usefulness, and all that may exist regardless of our knowledge.

This will lead us on towards a discussion of an individual and collective understanding of the world, in which the notions of conformity, continuity, and 'narrativity' are being used as instruments in the analysis of conceptions of the world and of culture. The role of hermeneutics in phenomenology is crucial for this discussion, and I will make use of Merleau-Ponty's theory of inter-subjectivity in terms of 'private world', 'social world' and 'perceived world', as there is a clear link to Husserl's ideas of the living-world, the ego, and inter-subjectivity behind these terms. When moving towards a possible use of phenomenology in dialogue, the ideas from Paul Ricoeur's more recent thinking will also be discussed.

Realism and Anti-Realism

The following discussion will lead towards the problem of how it is possible to relate a supposedly idealistic or anti-realistic view, i.e., Husserl's phenomenology, to van der Leeuw's phenomenology of religion, which claims the existence of an independent reality—god. The latter represents a sort of metaphysical realism. As we have seen, van der Leeuw keeps the question of god's real existence and of god's true nature away from human beings' perceptions of god. God is something totally different. Therefore it may be possible to approach the problem by distinguishing between the ontological and the epistemological questions. I will therefore proceed with my discussion by regarding the problem as one between a position of ontological realism and one of epistemological anti-realism. The position of ontological realism claims not only that a reality exists independent of us but also that we can justify our claims to knowledge by making reference to this reality. Without the completion of the latter claim, ontological realism would be of no interest. The position of epistemological anti-realism claims that there are no such things as evidence transcending truths in the sense of true statements; true statements can only be justified because they are based on evidence.[2] We must also ask whether the phenomenologies discussed did uphold this distinction, or whether we are faced with a combination between these two positions. This question will be of particular interest regarding van der Leeuw's idea of the phenomenology of religion.

What can be said about the phenomenological position/-s in terms of realism and/or anti-realism with regard to epistemological and ontological claims? Is it clear that Husserl's phenomenology represents an anti-realistic idealism on the level of epistemology? What can further be said about his ontological position? And can Heidegger be labeled as a representative of one or the other position? Is he approaching Daseins and entities from only one position, or would the analysis of Daseins imply a particular position while the analysis of entities would lead to another one?

With these questions in mind we will be able to approach the complexity of van der Leeuw's position/-s. This will lead towards a possible understanding of the shortcomings of his phenomenology of religion from a philosophical point of view. I am particularly thinking of his use of the notion of 'phenomenon' and the difference between that and the thinking of Husserl and Heidegger.

I will begin by presenting some definitions together with some problematic aspects from the analysis above, which will be helpful for the following discussion. The realist would say that the world consists of things and events which exist regardless of human beings and human knowledge. All things and events can be made objects of human knowledge. This understanding of existences independent of human knowledge will have an effect on the realists' arguments on the truth-value of statements. Statements have truth-value depending on facts existing independently of whether or not knowledge about them can be gained.

Anti-realism, which in one sense is a recent development of idealism, can be divided into a stronger and a weaker or softer version. According to the stronger

---

[2] Cf. Herrmann, 1996, p 12, 16.

version, a person can only have knowledge about their own conscious/mental experiences. The softer version would say that human knowledge consists of the knowledge of objects which have been constituted by human language, or through other cognitive abilities. In his work *Truth and Other Enigmas*, Dummett follows in principle the above definition of realism, when he formulates the opposition between realism and anti-realism. He does this by describing anti-realism as opposition to the realist's claim of objective truth-value, guaranteed by virtue of a reality independent of us. Dummett's contribution consists of redirecting the basis of the controversy away from the discussion of the existence of, and the reference to, entities towards whom we express our ideas by making statements—and of criteria for evaluating statements as true or false. By redirecting attention away from entities (the dispute in terms of existence and reference) to language, he lays the foundation for a debate on classes of statements (the disputed class) which can be said to be statements on a certain subject. In opposition to the realist, an anti-realist would argue "... that statements of the disputed class are to be understood only by reference to the sort of thing which we count as evidence for a statement of that class".[3]

In addition, we must also consider the statements on universals, and whether or not we are facing ideas which would lead to a realist account of universals or to a conceptualist view. Universals might be regarded as the general abstraction of a defined class of individuals belonging to it. Thus a perceived, particular, chair is not identical with its abstraction, the universal idea of the chair. The interesting point which we are to discuss is whether universals should be regarded as mental or mind-dependent, as has been suggested by conceptualists, or whether in phenomenology we are dealing with a realist understanding of universals as existing independently of any mind being aware of them.

As far as I can see, the discussion of ontological and epistemological realism/anti-realism will have to take the following into account:

Husserl: The status of the given in relation to conscious content as resulting from the phenomenological reduction. The distinction of the phenomenon between appearance and the appearing thing. The ontological difference between external and internal intentional objects according to the distinction between presentations and re-presentations in intentional acts.

Heidegger: The ontological difference between entity and being. The different aspects of the analysis of Daseins and entities. The distinction between 'world' and 'nature'.

van der Leeuw: The differentiation between God as the 'Subject' of religion, and God as a 'something'. The manifestation of something extra-worldy conceived of as an attribute of the adjective 'holy' to human beings or to natural objects, for example 'holy tree', 'holy water', etc.

The basic ideas of the phenomenon as that which appears of the temporal character of history, of intentionality, of the meaning of life, of essence, and of the method of reduction—epochē—are common to all three scholars.

---

[3] Dummett, 1992, 146.

Creating a Known World by World Perceptions

As stated above, I have chosen as my point of departure the problem of how phenomenology can create an opening for describing the human conception and incorporation of multiple flows of stimuli into consciousness. This means all the information stored as cognitive content that will be central to the establishment of a reality and thus central to a specific understanding of the world. This shows itself as world-view which in turn brings with it the problem of conformity and discrepancy between a personal and a collective world-understanding. There is also the problem of conformity and discrepancy between various collectively accepted world-views. The world-views emanate from a previously established understanding and interpretation of reality, i.e., the known world. With the word 'world' I want to cover all that exists or may exist, disregarding our possible knowledge thereof. 'Reality' consists of our acknowledgement of the world but it is not necessarily identical with the world in the sense that 'reality' covers the complete 'world'. Thus 'reality' means the elements of the world known to us— the known world.

Is my understanding of the world limited to the objects and relations known to me? And is it in any way constructive to talk about 'the surroundings' without human beings to reflect and talk about them? Is it at all, we may ask ourselves, fruitful to make a distinction between world and reality, where the world would be whatever exists regardless of people's inauguration of it into epistemic systems?

The distinction between world and reality concerns the difference between an antirealist's view, claiming that statements about the world can only be made in terms of our reality, and a realist's view, claiming that statements of the world are true or false independent of our knowing reality or not. My first, rough, interpretation of the antirealist view of the world would be this: the world is the reality, i.e., the sum of objects and relations known to the human mind and defined by linguistic terms. The tree, of course, only exists for us as our linguistic definition as 'tree'. However, saying that the tree exists only at an epistemic level is not, in my opinion, the same as claiming that the space-time relation defined by the word 'tree' does not exist independent of our ability to be aware of it. The realist position would claim that the tree exists independent of a knowing subject's possibility to perceive it or to have access to it.

The problem whether or not an object exists independent of the mind might be regarded by many people as rather an artificial issue. Most people are willing to accept, intuitively, the statement that an object exists regardless of our knowledge of it. But what about the more difficult and abstract things, or sense- or mind-dependent abstractions, such as the sense-datum 'red'. 'Red', or 'redness', is not identical with a particular shade of red, but it is regarded as a universal, as the class red to which all its variations belong. Does this class exist? The problem has to do with what we mean when we say that something exists, and on what conditions something exists and how we can gain knowledge of it. Discussions about God are no exceptions concerning this problem.

When philosophy deals with objects which we become aware of by perception, a distinction is made between material objects (physical objects and living bodies) and sensations/sense data. Material objects are different from sensations insofar as sensations are said to be immediate and private. Sensations are not held to have an external, physical existence. Material objects are considered as external time-space relations, as externally existing physical objects, to which access is public.

The distinction between material objects and sensations is important for understanding distinctions made in phenomenology between the different states of the objects of intentional acts. This is the point that Husserl makes by his distinction between external objects of perception and immanent objects, such as the ones of phantasies or hallucinations.

If the objects of awareness in one way or another depend on the individual's capacity to perceive them, as for example the sensations, the immediacy implied is not only an immediacy of awareness but given by the perceptual constitution itself.

Sensations, object awareness by means of the senses, such as seeing, hearing, touch, taste, smell are not only private, but also dependent on the complexity of relations between the sensory organ and external factors. We all know that, for instance, our abilities to perceive colour depends on certain physiological conditions in the eye, basically determined by the symbiotic functions of the 'rods' and the red, green and blue 'cones', and how their chemical contents exite the nerve-fibres in the eye in the process of light exposure. The nerve-fibres thus transmit specific impulses, in the form of electronic currents, to the brain. But colour is also wavelengths of light. The actual wavelength is in turn dependent on the surface structure of an illuminated object reflecting the incoming light of a specific wavelength. Therefore, when we become aware of a particular colour, being a property of an object, several conditions, both mental and non-mental, should be considered as the basis for this awareness.

The point is that there are many different factors, not only of an epistemic nature, but also, as shown in the example above, of a physiological nature that will influence our experience and perceptions of things and objects. All these factors can certainly colour subjectively our beliefs and statements on the states of affairs. Communication with other people therefore requires some mecanism that will allow us to modify our subjective views of the world by the exchange of ideas and perspectives. I will therefore discuss what phenomenology and the more recent contributions to the philosophical debate, from philosophers like Richard Rorty and Hilary Putnam, have to say on this. Before that I will, however, summarize what has been said so far.

The various ways of guaranteeing the reliability of our claims to a knowledge of particular objects and events founded on various forms of experiences carry both positive and negative aspects: the positions of realism or anti-realism generally held have their own problems. The position of realism has an obvious, positive aspect in the perspective of the religious person in particular, for whom it would in some forms liberate the mind from the burden of trying to find immanent proofs of the existence of a god—or several gods. This would be the case for the strongly metaphysical realist. This version would recognize our possibilities of expanding our knowledge by making statements on reality. It functions without proofs given according to established cognitive systems. In other words it would also consist of epistemological realism, i.e., of the position claiming that the world consists of things and events which exist indepent of us and our knowledge of them, and that we can, nevertheless, turn these into objects of knowledge. At its worst, this position could result in unreflected relativism, leading to a situation of propositional anarchy, where ideas and views of life can be had regardless of their intellectual integrity. In softer versions, ontological realism could end in an onto-logical relativism which would accept most ontological claims.

The opposing position, anti-realism, would accentuate our limited possibilities to make statements unless we can justify them by evidence. It would require some sort of intellectual integrity and honesty in relation to the claims made in a state-ment. Our running out of arguments, the anti-realist would not accept some hid-den card from up our sleeve as a final proof. In my opinion, the anti-realist posi-tion has the disadvantage of not supporting that which so many of us would intuitively express as "this cannot be all, there must be something else, something else, apart from what we know and can prove by means of cognitive systems of explanations". This becomes important when determining the conflict of whose explanatory model should be accepted.

However, the position of realism has its limitations too. The realist's positive account accepts our imaginative and innovative, cognitive ability to justify beliefs about mind-independent reality. However, the realist always runs the risk of being trapped in relativism or intellectual anarchy. One example of this is the religious pluralism in situations of religious dialogues where we might feel obliged to accept opposite positions and ideas instead of arguing against what we, in other situations, would refuse to accept since it contradicts our own views. This does not mean that a recognition of the plurality of views of life ought to be abolished for the benefit of ethnocentrism. It is important to provide the means and the opportunities for a communication of different views and also to allow free scope for criticism. The other position, i.e., of anti-realism, enforces our need to recog-nize the mind-dependency of our explanatory theories.

When dealing with most of the religious views of life we are concerned with beliefs in existing transcendent realities—god/s, spirits, etc.; beliefs which would clearly benefit from a position of ontological realism. We are also concerned with social communities in which the exhange of ideas is governed by sets of rules (descriptive schemes) which, to a large degree, are governed by epistemological anti-realism, i.e., they argue in favour of the mind-dependency of our explanatory theories. Is it then possible, taking the different nature of our questions into ac-count, to combine ontological realism in some sense with epistemological anti-realism? One of the problems here touches on the complexity of object awareness in perception and sensation. This is the problem of the adequacy of our claims. In the case of perception, the problem has to do with the public nature of the object awareness of material objects, and in the case of sensations, the problem relates to the immediacy of private awareness together with the uncertainty caused by the complex inter-dependency of internal and external conditions.

In both cases some kind of a sharing of impressions and perspectives must take place as a dialogue between individuals, if we want to find some sort of reliability, both with regard to our impressions and to the interpretation of our experiences.

Different Ways of Talking about Experience

The term 'experience' is ambiguous. It is a noun which refers both to an act and the content of the act. An experience, in terms of a specific act, can be public since it can be participated in by many at the same time, but this does not mean that the content, the experience gained, is equally shared. Let us use the holy communion as an example. The communion is shared by many other fellow Christians but it does not mean that everybody shares the same content although the experience of an act is shared. Furthermore, different Christian traditions profess different theological views of holy communion and this is a hindrance to share the altar.

An experience can thus contain both public and private aspects. When we reflect on object awareness, limiting ourselves to material objects, we nevertheless have to find some sort of common understanding which can be shared by most people despite these private aspects.

Experiences of sensations present another difficulty when the contents of these experiences are used to justify beliefs. I would explain this from the point of view of the content of the experience. Despite the privacy of, for example, dreams, we can have fruitful exchanges about them.

From the perspective of phenomenology I would claim that the basic problem is to determine the common features of the conscious content of experience described as remembered, imagined, perceived, etc. The problem arises from Husserl's claims that statements made by phenomenologists about phenomena are non-empirical. They are non-empirical in the sense that they do not require any verification from empirical experiences. This is the reason behind Husserl's argument that the natural attitude—that is the attitude towards the world envisaged by the empirical sciences—has to be bracketed. The sciences cannot guarantee a general epistemic certainty because they all present us with explanatory factual models from their own perspectives. According to Husserl, they are to be regarded as 'regional ontologies'. Even when all the different sciences are taken into account, each one of them gives at the most a reasonable account of reality, because none of them is wholly compatible with the other. What is needed is another way of looking at the entities of the world (the phenomena), i.e., another perspective from which they can be regarded as they appear in themselves. This attitude, which characterizes the phenomenological perspective, is proclaimed by the slogan: "To the things".

Now we may ask: what are the things, how do we gain knowledge (in one sense or another) of the things or the events in the world? What gives us the right to state anything whatsoever about the world?

It is now time to approach the problem of how to identify and communicate the entities of the world and our knowledge of them. I will treat these questions first in relation to the natural attitude and then in relation to Husserl's proposal(s). My starting-point is the idea that we must be able to communicate what we call knowledge, of whatever sort, in a manner that helps other people understand what we are trying to say. The acquisition of a language is therefore a central objective. There are, as we all recognize, different types of languages: ordinary, everyday languages and meta-languages, by which we try to explain the object-language in use. A mathematician, for example, can be said to use several languages: a daily language which is used in non-professional situations, like shopping (though maybe not when it comes to paying), an object-language when performing a calculation, and a meta-language when explaining the calculation. A major part of our lives consists of learning how to use and apply language, right from the time when a baby's guttural sounds are transformed to the word 'lamp'. (This development helps us making communication far more comfortable for, among others, aunts and uncles—of which I am one—although parents seem to be equipped with some mystic code that helps them understand the most weird sounds and to identify them as references to existing objects!) The central point is that the development of language is crucial in the process of incorporation into a social context, be it into the family or into society at large. This means that our languages consist of words which cannot be completely set free of our empirical attitude towards the surroundings in which we live. If our ideas and concepts have empirical causes and must be analysed in their empirical context, how then can reliability be approached from a point of view which completely neglects empirical circumstances?

Ought we to understand Husserl's request of a non-empirical attitude as some sort of 'tabula rasa' attitude, as a completely blank focusing of our vision on what he would call a 'perceptual horizon'? If so, how can we make what appears on that horizon comprehensible, first to ourselves and then to other people, when we try to communicate the impressions gained from our experiences? Maybe his proposal is much more trivial but phrased in a complicated manner. Maybe he means that we ought not to take it for granted that we have full access to an understanding of what we see? If the natural attitude means that perceptual objects are treated as facts, even by ordinary language, then he has a point in his observation that the basis of our cognition might be incomplete. He also has a point in his critique of empirical verificationalism, since there seems to be experiences which cannot be verified through sense-perception alone.

We should, according to Husserl, perceive the essences themselves. The essence cannot be said to be identical with the phenomenon, but the phenomenon consists of the essential features of the intentional object. In other words, a phenomenon is the appearance of its necessary essences (or properties) which makes it into what it is. Phrasing it in phenomenological terms: "A phenomenon is a unit of essential connections of a singular object". Thus the seeing of essences means the seeing of an object in its essential constituents, without which it would not be what it is. An essence is thus a necessary prerequisite for an object to be what it is, and an intentional object requires more than the essential feature which we can grasp in a single moment of perception. But how can we say anything about these essential features without references to an empirical reality? By taking into consideration Husserl's discussion on types, genus and species, we can see some of the problems of recognition of the invariable features of an object. In perception, the genus—which is the most general form of particular objects, such as trees—requires fewer necessary and invariable features than a species—such as a birch or an oak. Nevertheless, the problem remains of how to recognize these features so that they can be regarded as criteria of a phenomenon, when the empirical reference has been bracketed.

Husserl proposed to solve this problem by means of a reduction, by bracketing the empirically coloured presuppositions that might prevent us from seeing things as they are in themselves, when we rather see them as we *think* they are, or *expect* them to be. There are several instances of bracketing to take into account. One is the recognition of necessary and invariant features, discussed above. The process in which this takes place is known as ideation in Husserlian terms. Ideation consists of intuition into essence by suspending the matter of real existence. Neither every aspect of an object nor every side of a multisided object can be grasped in one singular act of perception. Let us take a house as an example. From a particular field of vision (horizon) I cannot observe more than two of its sides in one instant of seeing. Therefore, I cannot grasp its essence adequately since that would require a complete inspection, covering all sides at once. Grasping the essence adequately would require a return to the intentional object in several instances. This consciousness of objects by a one-sided experience of objects through sense-experience, such as seeing, is labeled 'empirical intuition'[4] by Husserl. This is distinguished from 'essential intuition' which is the consciousness not of the house as such, to follow up our above example, but of a something towards which our vision is directed; a something which occupies part of our visionary field.[5] The idea, or essence, is thus only what belongs to the object as it appears within the visionary field. From the aspect of empirical intuition, the object seen is a house, while from the aspect of essential intuition it is that which makes a house into a house. That which is perceived as a fact or a matter of facts by empirical sense experience (the house as a real existing object) is the given. It is this given that should be bracketed as a real existence. What appears in consciousness by essential intuition is then the self-givenness of the house, i.e., what in the end makes a house into a house and not into something else.

Earlier on I drew attention to two distinctions which are important to my analysis. The first one is the logical distinction between the phenomenon as appearance [Erscheinung] and the appearing thing, i.e., that which appears [Erscheinendes]. The second distinction is related to intentional acts, and it points out the distinction between the intentional object existing as an external reality and the intentional act, in which the intentional object is present as an immanent object of consciousness.

There is at least a logical difference between the appearance itself and the conscious content, i.e., the thing appearing in consciousness as a 'something' that

---

[4] Kockelmans, 1994, p 59.
[5] Kockelmans, 1994, p 59.

can become an object of recollection and thus be remembered as such. To remember something in terms of "I remember it as such" is the result of a mental act. All mental acts or acts of consciousness are intentional, according to Husserl, which means that being conscious always implies being conscious of something. This also indicates that, since the act is directed toward something, all consciousness always has a content or an object.[6] The object or content can refer to something which exists externally, but it can also be the case that the content or object only exists in consciousness, that it has an immanent presence. Husserl also makes the point that, with regard to what is given in consciousness, it does not matter, as far as the intentional object is concerned, whether the object presented is related to something externally existing or if it is only an object of imagination.

Let us return to the foundational role of experience for the establishment of knowledge. We have seen that Husserl recognizes that knowledge begins with experience, but that it does not remain within experience. This was his critique of the natural attitude and of the empirical sciences' account of knowledge. We may now ask whether Husserl himself succeeds in transcending experience as the foundation of knowledge. By bracketing the question of existence and the surrounding world, it seems that Husserl asserts that, whatever is, is not for it-self but for us, as conscious subjects. What matters as a basis for conscious recognition is thus only to be aware of something's presence in consciousness as an intentional object. As stated earlier, Husserl seems to regard knowledge as a cognitive act, as a reflection.

Let us consider 'ideation' as the most important act of 're-cognition'. What is being reflected on is the variations of one and the same intentional object, and the purpose is to determine the necessary invariant features, i.e., the essence. For this purpose we must have access to previous experiences of the same object stored in our memory in terms of chains of reminiscences, 'as such'. We can now also see what is meant by truth as a correspondence between the intentional object and its correlate. The latter is related to recollection. The problem is that recollection seems to me to be totally bound up with experience. This would go against Husserl's criticism of empiricism. Verification, by means of sense-experience, is not what binds the Husserlian understanding of knowledge to experience. The Husserlian idea of knowledge, it seems, does not limit verification to external experience alone. There are two interrelated notions which are important for my discussion on Husserl's notion of lived experience [Erlebnis] and the notion of the transcendental ego.

The notion of lived experience has, as we have seen, something to do with cognition as an act. Husserl either talks about a limited act of cognition related to a particular intentional act, or about consciousness in terms of an ongoing process. In the latter interpretation, which I support, 'lived experience' is not a singular event at a particular moment, but a total conscious content, as it is in a single moment. The process of testing variations takes place against the background of the total, conscious content. Let us move beyond Husserl for a moment and com-

---

[6] Kockelmans, 1994, p 18.

pare the notion of lived experience with the notion of 'life experience'. If 'Erleb-nis' is understood as life experience, it might facilitate the comprehension of how 'Erlebnis' relates to 'Erfahrung'. Experience as 'Erfahrung' will in one way or another always contribute to what we will recognize as our life experience. It also means that when a particular experience, 'Erfahrung', is mirrored against our total life experience, it is not identical with the latter but contributes to its expansion. If experience as 'Erlebnis' is regarded as our life experience, it might also provide us with the means to understand the notion of the 'transcendental ego' in contrast to that of the 'empirical ego'. The transcendental ego is the ego of both lived experience and life experience. This ego can never be the object of self-reflection, since it is always the subject of the total conscious content. The empirical ego, the ego of particular experiences [Erfahrungen] can become the Me of self-reflection, because it is possible to pick out particular events for reflection.

Husserl's distinction between the transcendental ego and the empirical ego will have consequences for the possibility of being essentially aware of another person. The other person is a transcendental ego, and since we cannot make our own transcendental ego the object of reflection, we will not be able to make another transcendental ego the object of our intentionality. What is open to reflection is the other person as an empirical ego as an object of empirical intuition. This means, according to Husserl, that inter-subjectivity will reside within the subjective sphere of the intending subject. Making consciousness the centre, in which all awareness of objects, ideas, imagination, etc. resides, makes it clear that Husserl advocates an epistemological anti-realism in the sense of the mind-dependency of every aspect of the conscious content. His request for a non-empirical foundation for cognition also indicates this position. As was seen above, Husserl argued against individual relativism, i.e., against the opinion that what is understood as the truth is always that which is true only for one individual. However, an oscillation can be observed between a position of ontological anti-realism and one of ontological realism. Firstly, I cannot see the difference between individual relativism and subjective idealism, where evidence is established as something self-evident, since the act of cognition always takes place within the consciousness of the individual subject. The remains of the intentional act have there as its correlate the complete conscious content known as life-experience. This would point towards ontological anti-realism. Secondly, even the known world will become a world of and for the subject, where the question of its real existence, i.e., of reality as existing independent of us, is bracketed. This indicates that Husserl could be advocating an ontological realism.

Martin Heidegger formulated a reaction against most of Husserl's cornerstones. First of all it is against the understanding of phenomenology. Important for this investigation is Heidegger's outlines of the conditions of the human dwelling in the world. His distinction between 'world' and 'nature', discussed earlier, is important when we deal with general analyses of the different epistemic and ontological positions of anti-realism and realism. Because of his world/nature distinction I regard him as an ontological realist in the sense that, according to him, nature—i.e., things and natural objects as extant entities—exists independent of human beings. The world is, as we saw, that which human beings know about nature. On an epistemic level I therefore suggest that Heidegger's position can be interpreted as one of anti-realism, since the known is conceived in terms of 'world' and is thus mind-dependent.

Further distinctions are crucial: (1) between 'being' as the constituent of everything that is, and 'being' as entity, (2) between the ontic and existentiell, the individual and temporal on the one hand, and, on the other hand, the ontological and existential, the general and a-temporal, time-transcending, and (3) between the possible attitudes of inauthenticity and authenticity.

Can 'being' be experienced? Since Heidegger does not regard 'being' [Sein] as an entity, as something that is, the answer has to be no. The particularity of human existence—Dasein—complicates the question because of Heidegger's definition of 'being' in relation to Dasein and to other entities: Dasein is the entity which can reflect on its own 'being'. Does this contradict my suggested proposition? Maybe not, if what can be reflected on, experienced, is not 'being' [Sein] in itself but our particular way of existing which Heidegger calls 'Eksistenz'. Thus, I cannot experience my 'being', but I can to some degree experience 'what' I am and 'how'. The 'what' and 'how' presuppose 'being', because they are caused by 'being' but do not themselves cause being.

The opposite of 'being' is death. Death is 'non-being'. We cannot experience our own death, but only the death of other people. This point is central to Heidegger's view. We are equally unable to experience our own 'being', but I propose that, by analogy, we can gain some insight into our own 'being' by experiencing the 'being' of other people. In that way we can gain insights for ourselves into what 'being' is and also death's actual consequences. Some people may argue against the idea that we cannot experience our own death by making a reference to so-called Near Death Experience (NDE). I disagree because of the N(ear) of the NDE. A person with such an experience was close to death but did not actually die. As I see it, Heidegger makes the point that death is inevitable and insights gained from the experience of other peoples' deaths force us to reflect on the fragility and precariousness of life, and to choose our own way of life more responsibly.

In relation to the impossibility fully to experience and understand one's own being, Heidegger stresses the insight into existential phenomena of (other people's) deaths, guilt, care, love, etc. as the only authentic way of approaching one's own existence.

Compared to Husserl, Heidegger proposes a different idea of intentionality. For him intentionality is not, as for Husserl, a mental act—i.e., the directing of one's own consciousness, the immanent 'intentio'—towards an 'intentum' of inner perception. Rather, intentionality is directly connected with Dasein's being-in-the-world and entry into the world. As we have seen, Heidegger commented on two different, erroneous uses of the word 'intentionality', one of which means that both the intending, perceiving subject and the intended, perceived object are regarded as world-objects in the sense that both are conceived of as extant entities. Heidegger regards this as the objectivizing of intentionality. A particular Dasein is always at some intentional stage, because, in the mode of being-in-the world, it is directed toward the world. The Dasein cannot therefore step out of its own being and make itself an extant entity.

Commenting on the other, in Heidegger's view, misunderstanding of intentionality, he actually criticizes Husserl's basic understanding of intentionality. When relating the intentional object only to consciousness, intentionality becomes subjectivized. According to Heidegger, this is a complete misunderstanding of intentionality since Heidegger regards intentionality as always concerning the extant.

Intentionality firstly has to do with world-entry, with the incorporation of entities of nature into the world, and secondly with the handling of the entities of the world, which have become present, as 'present-at-hand'. Intentionality in this second sense transforms the present object into an object present in possible functions, i.e., into an entity which can be grasped in the sense of 'readiness-at-hand'.

In perception a possible extant entity, given by world-entry, becomes a real extant entity because of its availability. What intentionality presents us with through perception, must in one way or another be explained by opening up its functions. For that reason, hermeneutics becomes central to Heidegger's thinking. The hermeneutical process provides us first of all with the difference between the being of Dasein and the being of entities. This is done by means of a self-interpretation of one's own being which, according to Heidegger, can only be performed by Daseins. The self-interpretation consists of reflection on the human 'Eksistenz' as being-in-the-world. This, to Dasein exclusive, possibility of self-reflection helps us grasp the ontological difference. Hermeneutics also reveals what I call the second aspect of the ontological difference, namely that Dasein's being may be disclosed as something apparently different from what it appears to be. In other words, Dasein might show itself as reluctant to identification by conventional ideas and praxis. The meaning of 'Eksistenz', springing from this continuous analysis of our relationship of being-in-the-world with others, is revealed and manifested through speech, 'logos', i.e., how we put things into words.

Thus hermeneutics has two implications of ontological difference; first the reflection of oneself in relation to the things and objects of the world, i.e., discovering, and then the mirroring of one's own Dasein against other Daseins, i.e., being discovered. This also implies that it is always 'being' which is discovered, i.e., which constitutes phenomena. But we may distinguish between two different types of phenomena; both the phenomenon of being a particular entity, and the phenomenon of Dasein's being in general. I have labelled the former 'existentiell phenomena' and the latter 'existential phenomena'. Since, in both cases, phenomena have to do with 'being', we can see why Heidegger can maintain that there is nothing behind phenomena. If there was something behind phenomena, it would turn us back to 'onto-theology'. Behind 'being' there is nothing. At the same time, this statement is a refutation of Kant's distinction between reality, as we perceive it, and reality in itself. For Heidegger, this is an impossibility, since we always perceive what there is to perceive. His distinction is instead one between an entity being-at-hand and an entity not-at-hand.

I have stated earlier that van der Leeuw understands phenomenology in a more limited way than Husserl and Heidegger do. His focus is only on religion, i.e., on the interpretation of expressions of experiences that are different in kind from experiences of the world because the former contains an extra-worldly manifestation of something totally extraordinary. But besides this, we also find the idea of religion, according to which there would be no human existence, nor culture, without religion.[7] If this is the case, van der Leeuw's approach cannot be related only to Husserl's or Heidegger's views. van der Leeuw's approach would imply that the study of religious experiences is also the study of the foundations of human existence. By bracketing the question of the existence of God by ontological reduction, which van der Leeuw urges us to do, his phenomenology of religion risks being transformed into anthropology, i.e., the phenomenon of religion becomes an immanent human construction without reference to any independently existing reality. This he tries to overcome, not by denying the anthropological aspect, but by demanding that religion can only be studied from inside itself. Among other things, it has to do with his idea that on the one hand we do not know what God is and on the other hand that whatever is said about God is what it means to religious people. Thus, the scholar is only able to understand religion if they are religious persons.[8] It is precisely in this light that I have described van der Leeuw's use of epochē as limited. His phenomenology does obviously not follow Husserl's demand for presuppositionlessness.

I suggested earlier that van der Leeuw's phenomenology of religion could be intrepreted as: 1) a systematization of data in line with Chatepie de la Saussaye's understanding of the phenomenology of religion, 2) a hermeneutic of lived experiences, following the hermeneutic and psychological traditions of Dilthey, Heidegger, Spranger, Jaspers and Binswanger, and 3) a general phenomenology, applied by the phenomenologists themselves, so that phenomenology becomes a way of living.[9]

The three aspects of the phenomenology of religion can be said to correspond to three different kinds of understanding. The first one can be said to be in fact related in the sense that one has to understand what is an expression of a religious experience apart from other experiences. In van der Leeuw's phenomenology this is connected with 'eidetic vision' or 'ideation'. The second aspect is understanding in the hermeneutical sense of [Verstehen], which is focused on other people's experiences of others, i.e., on their expressions of their dwelling in the world and their coping with reality. This provides an outline of what life is and thus leads to the third level of understanding, which is the understanding of oneself.

The two latter forms of understanding in van der Leeuw's phenomenology relate to a complicated mixture of experiences of understanding. It seems to be the result of different influences from both Husserl, Dilthey, and Heidegger.

As we have seen, Husserl made the distinction between access to the experiences made by the empirical ego (as in the phrase "then I did this"), i.e., to the reference to oneself when accounting for an event, and by the transcendental ego

---

[7] cf. Waardenburg, 1978, p 211, 232n.
[8] cf. Waardenburg, 1978, p 236.
[9] cf. Waardenburg, 1978, p 224.

which cannot be experienced as such, because it is the ego that expresses the 'I' itself.

Husserl maintains that the other person can only be experienced in terms of their own expressed, empirical ego. Other people's experiences are not mine, because I only have access to their expression of what was experienced and/or I can see the results of their experiences through their acts.[10]

Waardenburg has pointed out that van der Leeuw was of the opinion that there was no difference in observing the ego of oneself or the ego of another person. The difference is solely in the act.[11] Furthermore, it is clear that van der Leeuw also uses another notion of experience, namely the notion of 'primal experience' [Ur-erlebnis]. This experience is inaccessible, but it can be understood by the hermeneutics of experiences, which reconstructs primal experiences. As far as I can see, the notion of 'primal experience' corresponds to Husserl's 'Erlebnis' in the sense that both notions refer to events within a specific moment ('now'), after which they cannot be fully recaptured in their originality. van der Leeuw therefore states that we have no immediate access to our own lives. Primal experiences must be reconstructed. Life is, furthermore, always the life of an individual person, their own reality, their personal history. Against this background I am prepared to say that we can observe an obvious similarity between van der Leeuw and Husserl with regard to the notion of the transcendental ego. That ego reflects on ordinary experiences by recollecting expressions. It is also possible to compare their use of the notion 'empathy' and the question of genuine access to other people's life-experiences. Here Husserl seems clearer of the limited possibilities of understanding the other person. For him 'empathy' is a strictly epistemic term. van der Leeuw stresses instead the real opportunity to enter somebody else's experiences through reconstruction. For him, 'empathy' is also a psychological term.

Religious phenomena are constituted by experience and are accessible through expressions of experience. This follows from van der Leeuw's idea that phenomenology begins with somebody giving an account of an experience. We have also seen that religious experience involves a supreme being as an active agent, as the Subject of religion. This Subject cannot be fully understood or identified. Religion cannot be understood on the basis of its metaphysical foundation, i.e., not from its access to God, but only from human expressions of human experiences. According to van der Leeuw, we can only understand religion from a human perspective. I feel personally great sympathy with this point. However, the status of revelation is unclear in his thinking. It is only the individual person's account of what has been revealed to them that is a phenomenon which can be studied. This corresponds well to his idea of what phenomenology is.[12] However, it is difficult to see how this can be combined with his metaphysical ideas of God as the Subject of revelation.

Is this now correct: a person's expressed experience is a phenomenon? van der Leeuw explicitly says that phenomena are made known to us when the expres-

---

[10] Cf. Kockelmans, 1994, p 291, 279, 288.
[11] Waardenburg, 1972, p 164, cf. Waardenburg, 1978, p 225f.
[12] Cf. Waardenburg, 1978, p 233f.

sions are named in accordance with some understanding of what is being expressed. Expression is made by means of our construction of ideal types which are used as normative criteria, so that we can typify and structure those expressions which we have appointed as religious phenomena.

This indicates that, according to van der Leeuw, the phenomenon is only accessible on the epistemic level, since it is an immanent construction, like Husserl's phenomena. However, phenomena also seem to point at some mind-independent reality, since religious experiences involve a transcendent, metaphysical agent. On the epistemic level, this indicates a position of anti-realism (God is only known through our images of God). On the ontological level it indicates a position of metaphysical realism (van der Leeuw takes it for granted that God exists independent of us).

Considering the notion of phenomenon, which should be defined against the notion of understanding [Verstehen], we have seen that van der Leeuw's use can be interpreted in two ways. One has to do with experience. In this case the experience of an appearance involves the actions of a metaphysical reality, of the Subject as an active agent together with the experiencing subject. That which appeared in the experience could not, as we have seen, be referred to fully in itself, because of our limited possibility to give an account of the active agent. This experience is in one sense a phenomenon. If we make use of Husserl's distinction between phenomenon as appearance [Erscheinung]—which is the act in which an appearance is experienced—and the phenomenon as the appearing thing [Erscheinendes]—which is the conscious content of the experience—then van der Leeuw can be said to use the word 'phenomenon' meaning 'Erscheinung' when talking about the appearance of the active agent. But, as we have seen, van der Leeuw also claims, as Heidegger does, that "there is nothing behind the phenomenon", and also that revelation is not in itself a phenomenon. Only someone's account of the revelation can be a phenomenon for reflection. This indicates that, when it comes to his idea of phenomenology, he moves from regarding the phenomenon as appearance (the actual experience of something appearing) to the expression of the experience, i.e., to the conscious content of the experience. Regarding the phenomenon as an expression, van der Leeuw maintains that there is nothing behind the phenomenon. In the act of phenomenological interpretation, an attempt is made at interpreting somebody's expressions of an experience, so that the expressed meaning, i.e., the life-understanding of the person involved, can be grasped and understood by the phenomenologist. But it does not end here. During the process of reconstruction the researcher shares, according to van der Leeuw, the life-condition with the other person so that the actual meaning-content will be shared by the researcher as well, because the reconstructed experience will become the experience of the researcher, too. The shared experience will thus result in a shared self-understanding, i.e., the acceptance that we can only be saved by divine grace.

This understanding [Verstehen] is expressed through speech or, as van der Leeuw puts it, by giving testimony. Thus it creates a basis for a phenomenon which can be interpreted. So we move within a hermeneutical circle similar to the one we found in Heidegger's work. However, their hermeneutic circles lead to different results. In Heidegger's case we remain within the realms of being-in-the-world, where we strive for the fullness of 'being' through our response to existential phenomena. For van der Leeuw, the hermeneutical circle looks much the same but the hermeneutics of (a) existential phenomena expressed in terms of historicity lead to (b) the insight into the limitation of being, by pointing out the need for salvation by divine grace, which again (c) points back to the historicity of human existence. We may now ask what this divine grace consists of, and how we can have any sort of knowledge of it.

Knowing and Recognizing

Inspired by Graham Ward, I will now discuss the following question: "How can anything be known without it also being recognized?". The fundamental philosophical problem in dealing with religion and religious statements has to do with the status of the claim that humans are being addressed by something wholly other and beyond ordinary knowledge. Graham Ward has phrased the problem in the following manner: "How can anything be known without it also being recognized? How can there be a wholly other who addresses us?"[13] In other words: how can I, as a religious believer, express the knowledge I have gained from my experiences claiming that my statements are true though they transcend evidence?

Let us start with some problems that are caused by philosophical distinctions. First there is the one between epistemology and ontology and then there is the one between realism and anti-realism.

Religious belief in some metaphysical reality requires a realist's position at the ontological level. At the same time some sort of epistemic 'fair play'—which does not allow people of faith to make religious statements which cannot be scrutinized in the same manner as other statements—is required from a philosophical point of view. This has been the central point of challenge to religion by the logical positivists during this century. Some sort of anti-realism at the epistemic level is thus required, i.e., a position according to which we should not accept evidence transcendent statements as statements true to facts.

Various solutions have been suggested to the question. One is the distinction between 'truth' regarded as correspondence in an empirical sense, and 'truth' understood in epistemic terms of adequacy, in a psychological sense. Another solution means regarding religious statements as statements formulated by a special language (the religious language) where the statements are regarded as metaphors. Yet another solution means giving up the whole problem by claiming that philosophy has completely misunderstood religion and that religion does not involve the question of truth, but is only concerned with meaning.

I regard that solution as the most desperate one. It is, although very attractive, very complicated. Most people would surely agree that religious belief has to do with meaning. Religious practice has a meaning-giving function, both for the

---

[13] Ward, 1995, p 20.

participating individual and for the community. This practice includes acts, statements etc.—what Dilthey calls the 'objective spirit' which comprises the multitude of manifested inner experiences of the human spirit objectivated through bodily activities, and as results of actions.[14]

In my opinion, these actions, activities and statements, coming from the believer, should be open to scrutiny from the perspective of truth-claims. The problem as I see it, is that religious life and practice concern both experiencing meaning, and also the proclamation of ultimate truth, i.e., the proclamation of the existence of a transcendent, divine reality. Thus we are back at square one again. It is interesting to notice that this problem seems less important for the believer than for the philosopher of religion. Is it therefore only an academic problem? I would not think so, and I agree with Herrmann that the problem is given by the tension between epistemological anti-realism which concerns claims about our world and metaphysical realism which concerns claims about an independent world.[15]

As I see it, this problem can only be solved by a modification of a much too polarized dichotomy between the two positions. As long as we stick to this distinction in its strong sense, the philosophical problem will remain of how to combine a belief in an independently existing divine reality with a demand to avoid evidence transcendent true statements. Before entering that discussion, I will point out an interesting observation on the use of metaphors and the acceptance of metaphorical language. This is also the reason why I am not willing to regard religious life and practice as only a matter of meaning.

There are occasions when we would like to talk about an object, or tell people about a situation in words which go beyond mere facts. If somebody asks me about the woman I love, I might want to add something that says something about my feelings that is more than a mere clinical description; something like: "She is a rose in full bloom". Then everybody knows that she is not a rose, but as they also know something about the beauty of roses, they do not think I am utterly mad. Some might even say that I have used a very poetic language.

Poetry contains metaphors for the purpose of enriching an otherwise poor language, so that we can see beyond the mere words. A good poem can express a multitude of complex feelings and expressions without accounting for anyone in particular. Poetic language helps us see things beyond the ordinary meaning of the words by observing the different contexts in which words are applied. Heidegger points out that, in many cases, existential phenomena can only be approached through poetry. He also claims that poetry is the prime language of philosophy.

Poetry also plays an important role in religion. We all know of the appreciation of poetry within Islam, and the function of poetically formulated riddles in Zen Buddhism, which, when meditated on, bring about sudden illuminations, 'satori'.

But poetry does not give direct access to the unknown or the unrevealed. It functions as a mediator. Through poetry we are able to see things differently.

---

[14] Cf. Dilthey, 1977, p 126f. See also *Vår tids filosofi*, 1987, p 34.
[15] Herrmann, 1995b, p 115f. Cf. Herrmann, 1995a, p 93.

Poetry does not undergo the scrutiny of philosophers because, as I see it, they know about the limited claims of poets. Even if poetry has a clear role within religious language, it is not possible to reduce religious language into poetry. Religious texts should not only be regarded as texts aiming at clarifying and opening up states of mind. Some texts also have the function of articulating something about reality. Let us take the Christian creed as an example. Here we have texts that consist of metaphors combined with straightforward propositions in ordinary language. The main purpose is to declare belief in the triune God, the creator, redeemer, and sanctifier of heaven and earth. As Christians we profess belief in a transcendent deity.

The problem defined by Ward's questions concerns the distinction between a transcendent divine reality and our images of it, or between God and our images of God. This is the same problem that van der Leeuw observed. The problems of truth-claims will occur particularly when this distinction is not observed, i.e., when believers equate God with the images or impressions of God formulated by humans. I do not mean that this observance would solve the problem, nor that there is a final solution to the problem, which is as old as religion itself. I am only indicating that, by taking on the responsibility for our own images and ideas without transforming them into divinity, we might have a better opportunity to exchange the perspectives behind them in genuine dialogue with others. Whatever God is, I do not know, but I might have an opportunity to discover how we imagine God by studying the various expressions we use about God.

Philosophers like Richard Rorty and Hilary Putnam are trying to overcome the dichotomy between realism and anti-realism. They share the same reasons but use different arguments. Both seem to regard the distinction as philosophically superfluous, since it creates problems rather than solves them. Rorty argues in favour of 'pragmatic ethnocentrism' by adopting an anti-representationalist account of the relation between natural science and the rest of culture. This account views knowledge as "a matter of acquiring habits of action for coping with reality".[16] The pragmatic liberal ethnocentrism, which is the end of Rorty's anti-representationalism, opens up the field for an encounter between different cultures. This openness to others is, according to him, part of the self-image of the liberal ethnocentrism.[17] I understand Rorty's ethnocentrism, not in the sense of exclusiveness favouring a particular ethnic group or nation, but rather as an acceptance or recognition of a cultural determination, which means that we cannot transcend the culture to which we belong. In my case it would be the western culture. This idea of ethnocentrism also stresses the recognition and the acceptance of other people's cultural determination. Rorty says, that in our encounter with others:

> All we should try to do is to get inside the inhabitants of that culture long enough to get some idea of how we look to them, and whether they have any ideas we can use. That is also all they can be expected to do on encountering us.[18]

---

[16] Rorty, 1994, p 1.
[17] Rorty, 1994, p 2.
[18] Rorty, 1994, p 212f.

I sympathize with this idea, but what does it presuppose? Unless we are familiar with our own culture, how can we possibly know if an outside observer's comments and possible advice are of relevance to us? Does it mean that it is just a matter of reading one's own ideas into another context? Taking Rorty's idea to the extreme (not claiming that this is what he demands) I wonder if it is possible to grasp what is labelled as the western culture in general. Personally I have problems enough to cope with my own limited sphere of my 'western' culture. Gaining enough knowledge to be able to orient myself within my own society limits my options of being a cosmopolitan. However, I do not dismiss Rorty's idea as such, because I think he has made an important point by indicating the role that cultural determination plays in our meetings with other people. This I will come back to when discussing attitudes, in particular the phenomenological attitude.

Putnam makes a different point. Let us return to the question: "How can anything be known without it also being recognized?". In *Reason, Truth and History*, Putnam presents two philosophical perspectives, where one relates to metaphysical realism. 'Truth', according to this perspective which Putnam calls the 'externalist' one, means some sort of correspondence between "words or thought-signs and external things and sets of things".[19] He sees this perspective in contrast to an 'internalist' view. According to this, referential questions only make sense within theories or mind-dependent descriptions.[20] Thus correspondence cannot be independently tested. The notions which refer a linguistic item to a non-linguistic item are, according to Putnam, internal to our understanding of the world. This is the basis for Putnam's move from mere 'internalism' to 'internal realism'. What he calls 'internalism' is very similar to Dummett's 'non-realism' or 'anti-realism'.

According to Putnam, the externalist perspective (metaphysical realism) presents two hopeless cases. One consists of taking a "God's eye point of view" that guarantees truth by conditions which are not mind-dependent. The other one does not leave the already known, and is therefore not constructive, when the reality of a metaphysical object or thing is referred to by negation of its mind-dependent counterpart. This would mean that no new knowledge is added. We are only informed of what is not the case.

Putnam's point is that internalism is contextual, that signs and objects have their field of reference according to the 'scheme of description' of a particular context. In my mind, what makes up for the realism of his internal realism is the acceptance of the multitude of unified cultural as well as scientific contexts, although considering their relative differences as classes of contextual fields in the world. Thus it is the world that, according to Putnam, guarantees Self-Identifying-Objects, since the experience of an object always has an external side which does not depend on the will. This has consequences for our ways of explaining truth. Truth and rational acceptability are interdependent notions because we are de-

[19] Putnam, 1990, p 49.
[20] Putnam, 1990, p 49.

pendent on the context in which and against whose rules (the scheme of description) a statement is made. Putnam suggests the following definition: *"a statement is true of a situation just in case it would be correct to use the words of which the statement consists in that way in describing the situation"*.[21] Putnam also holds that a statement can be justified if the words used to describe the situation are used according to the context-dependent scheme of description. Does this open up for metaphysical references? I mean: if language (the use of words) is used properly according to the contextual rules, what then would hinder metaphysical realism as characterized above? I believe Putnam would answer these questions by pointing at the use of contextually accepted rules for the possible usages of words. Any particular statement must therefore be mirrored against other descriptive statements of a particular situation which are accepted as true. From a position of metaphysical realism, for instance, making reference to a transcendent divine and independently existing reality for the purpose of justifying a religious belief can thus imply a lack of awareness of the limiting functions of the rules of description, according to the contextual scheme in which the statement was made. This is at least Putnam's case, as I read him. He does not argue specifically about religious statements. However, I would interpret him as claiming that religious statements can be true since a statement being true does not require justification here and now, even if it is not free from all justification since the claim indicates that the statement ought to be justifiable at some point.[22] It could happen that in dialogue with me a person from a context different from mine might argue according to other rules which I could successfully translate into my language and accept as new or as completing guiding rules.

Both Rorty and Putnam represent pragmatism. Rorty holds the position of ethnocentrism, which represents a form of relativism, by arguing that a specific culture's own rules for truth and justification cannot be used in a context of inquiry other than one's own. Putnam's pragmatism (internal or pragmatic realism), seems in some way to be similar to that of Rorty, even though they both claim to hold different positions.[23] The whole issue depends on how Putnam's understanding of context, in the sense of a scheme of description, should be interpreted. Rorty's interpretation is that Putnam stresses a holistic position, while Rorty himself holds a relativist position. If Putnam regards the scheme of description as the only one presently accepted, which would go against my reading of him, then his opinion is very different from Rorty's opinion, since Rorty clearly stresses that the world consists of different cultural wholes which on the epistemic level are to a large extent incompatible. Putnam seems to underline that the scheme of description is one, though it is not static and not universally accepted, but open to reform. Although governed by the scheme of description, there are many different ways of using words, even incompatible ones, but as long as we accept the rules for justification we are in no major trouble, taking into account Putnam's claim that:

[21] Putnam, 1992, p 115.
[22] Putnam, 1990, p 56.
[23] Cf. Putnam, 1990, p 216, 1992, p 69, 109f. Rorty, 1994, p 24f.

We can only hope to produce a more rational *conception* of rationality or a better *conception* of morality if we operate from *within* our tradition ..., but this is not at all to say that all is entirely reasonable and well with the conceptions we now have. We are not trapped in individual solipsistic hells, but invited to engage in a truly human dialogue; one which combines collectivity with individual responsibility.[24]

This leads on to my final chapter, which will deal with the question of what kind of role phenomenology can have within religious studies.

[24] Putnam, 1990, p 216.

CHAPTER 6

An Alternative Role for Phenomenology within Religious Studies

Coming to the end of this book, I will now try to formulate an alternative use of phenomenology within religious studies. My aim is not to substitute what is traditionally labelled the 'Phenomenology of Religion', but I want rather to present a modified understanding for the purpose of making phenomenology applicable in a wider context. The modifications I suggest aim at showing that phenomenology may be a method for approaching specific questions which occur generally. In this sense, phenomenology is focused on the words 'meaning', 'understanding' and 'intentional something', and it does not depart from the basic components of phenomenology in general. The differences will have more to do with our approaching questions of meaning, understanding and intentional objects and the purpose for which we apply a phenomenological method. What I have in mind is promoting dialogue both between individuals and groups with different views of life as well as between different sciences and/or scholarly disciplines using a phenomenological method.

The modifications I suggest will be concerned with the methodological concepts which we have met with in the previous chapters, and my discussion will thus focus on presuppositionlessness as the basic attitude and bracketing as the method against the background of this question: "How far can we go before we reach a point where dialogue about perspectives between individuals, representing different views of life and different contexts, becomes meaningless?".

There are obvious risks that presuppositionlessness and bracketing might be observed to such an extent that we do not allow our own perspective to contribute to the dialogue or that we dare not question attitudes and solutions championed by our opponent. Nevertheless, these two methodological concerns are crucial to the construction of a pragmatic phenomenology, that is, to a phenomenology with a more human face than the romanticism we sometimes find implicit in declarations of phenomenological attitudes. Even so, I want to hold on to the idea that phenomenology provides us with fundamentally important insights for our self-understanding through our meeting with others who do not share our ideas and perspectives. In this process we continuously expand our views of life and thus our understanding of the world, i.e., of our world-view as a human construction.

Presuppositionlessness through Bracketing

We have seen in the analyses of Husserl, Heidegger and van der Leeuw that their understanding of the world and of human relations to the world are vital to their views on phenomenology. For Husserl as well as for van der Leeuw, it is in our relation to the world, in terms of knowledge and understanding, that the attitude of presuppositionlessness should be observed. The reasons are easy to understand; the observation of presuppositionlessness by a bracketing of judgements provides an open attitude towards internal and external appearances.

Normally we support an attitude of being free from presuppositions, if we by presuppositions mean an unwillingness to learn and maybe to change attitudes or perspectives. But we may ask to what length this attitude can be taken before we become people who seem to lack opinions and ideas of a kind without which dialogue between individuals and groups cannot take place.

I have sometimes been fortunate enough to participate in inter-religious dialogues. Many times, though, a willingness to enter into dialogue has been secured by avoiding conflicts on the agenda. Such dialogues can easily become inter-religious monologues. Such agendas represent an attitude of negative presuppositionlessness, where an unfortunate confusion of the issues on the agenda with (tactical) politeness seems to have taken place. When I now propose that the attitude of presuppositionlessness should be observed, I want to promote it as a precaution against ignorance and prejudice. Bracketing, epochē, should not be a suspension of our ideas and views of life but should rather be a temporary suspension of the claims of our statements about states of affairs as the unshakable basis for our ideas. This is, as I interpret it, the weaker form of bracketing. In other words, I do not support the Husserlian understanding of bracketing, i.e., the bracketing of the natural attitude and the 'Umwelt'. In his case, it was for the sake of finding certain knowledge. That strict application of epochē, however, would leave us without basic perspectives for a fruitful exchange of ideas through dialogue.

The prerequisites for the phenomenology I have in mind is the acknowledgement of the fundaments of one's own knowledge, views of life and of self-understanding. In this case presuppositionlessness is expressed as an understanding and recognition of pluralism, and bracketed should be the judgement that one's own claims are the only true and indisputable ones.

Empathy and Intersubjectivity

Phenomenology for dialogue contains a strong element of interpretation. Hermeneutics will be an important part in the formation of knowledge through the phenomenology I advocate. I do not intend to copy the hermeneutical phenomenology of van der Leeuw, because of the problems of what is sometimes called the phenomenological attitude. Such an attitude can be described as follows:

> It is an attitude that enfolds both the interpreter and his object of interpretation and that enables the interpreter to leave his own world for a moment, cross into the world of the 'other', and return with a knowledge made possible by his crossing.[1]

Problems connected with this attitude make me hesitant to accept certain ideas of phenomenology, for example the assumption that we can actually surpass our own reality, our own knowledge, and enter the world of the other person. In a Husserlian perspective, the notion of empathy cannot be understood in this sense.

[1] Brenneman, Yarian and Olson, 1982, p 1.

This is so because the transcendental ego cannot be made an object for reflection. It is only the expressed experiences of the empirical egos that can be made objects for reflections in relation to other people. Heidegger would also question this attitude because it would mean (at least as I read it) that we copy another Dasein. Following Heidegger, we would become 'das Man'. Now one aspect of Heidegger's idea of how and why we must exist in relation to others is that we can learn something which can help us in our choice of how to live and how to act in particular situations. Another, and a more fundamental, aspect of our relation to others is 'to-be-with' [Mit-Sein] that is Dasein's fundamental and common way of being. 'To-be-with' means basically: care. This care also consists of self-dignity. We also saw the possibility of relating our existentiell situations to human history. 'Historicity' in Heidgger's thinking cannot be said to express the attitude quoted above. That could again be an expression of 'das Man'. Through the examples of other people, history in the sense of historicity provides us with the option of mirroring experiences and situations which require a choice on my part.

As we have seen, van der Leeuw is rather unclear about his phenomenological attitude. Phenomenology supports his idea of reconstruction through an interpolation of the phenomenon into one's own life as experience. On the one hand, van der Leeuw maintains that the conscious content of experiences in this process does not differ from one person to another. On the other hand, life always consists of one's own reality, of one's personal history.

Is another phenomenological attitude, which does not emphasize this self-transcendence, possible? I would say so, and such a phenomenological attitude would also emphasize on understanding but not without consideration of the limitations for understanding both oneself and other people.

The basic point of departure for this phenomenology is the fact that as human beings we seem to have a lot in common. This opportunity is expressed when we approach existential phenomena, such as death, love, hate, guilt, etc. But it does not imply that our solutions to life's various situations are identical. Nevertheless, experiences of existential problems and the solutions we embrace can be brought into dialogue.

For this purpose it is important to qualify what we mean by 'world'. Merleau-Ponty has suggested that 'world' ought to be interpreted from at least two different aspects: one is the private world, the world of feeling and perception. The problems of the private world arise from the privacy of experiences in terms of sensations. What I perceive cannot be so completely objectified that it loses its subjectivity. The subjectivity can be interpreted in some sort of 'solipsism' that cannot be completely reduced. However, there is also always a wish that what I see or feel should also be seen or felt by the other person.[2] Inter-subjectivity is dependent on successful communication. This leads on to the second aspect, i.e., the social world in which otherness reveals itself in conflicts of interest. These conflicting interests are controlled by collectively approved norms and laws.[3]

[2] Hamrick, 1987, p 28f.
[3] Hamrick, 1987, p 29.

Since there are different sets of norms and laws, there can also be conflicts of interests within and between different social worlds. Inter-subjectivity means, according to Merleau-Ponty, that I should strive for a "living unity of objectivity and subjectivity in the relationships I have with others and the world around me".[4] In other words, we should always support efforts which will promote views of life which consider both the needs of the individual and the needs of the community, such as freedom of speech, religious freedom, the right to be different (due to abilities, colour, ethnic belonging, etc). In my interpretation, this can only be done by means of communication founded on dialogue. That is also stressed by Ricoeur and Jeanrond.

To Ricoeur, the risk of cultural onesidedness can only be overcome through dialogue, where the different evaluations of particular experiences are discussed. One such topic could be the need for Muslim workers (living in a non-Muslim context like Sweden for example) to leave work in order to participate in communal prayer on Fridays. Another example is the question whether religion should be regarded as a private concern or a public concern. The aim of dialogue is to find a probable interpretation of a situation, a text, etc. that would be accepted by other people: "... an interpretation must not only be probable, but more probable than another".[5] Or as Jeanrond has put it, we need each other for the purpose of correcting our individual perspectives, and to become self-critical. If not, we might face the risk of isolationism and ethnocentrism, expressed as: "Mind your own business!".

According to Ricoeur, the world consists of the surrounding reality which is defined by the living speech, by the act of expressing of ourselves. Texts, written accounts of the world, are in his opinion accounts of quasi-worlds. The world of a text is closed. It does not point at the real world, at reality. For this to take place the text, or rather the meaning or the world of the text, must be opened up by the speech-act of an actual person, taking part in, and letting themselves be engaged in, the text. The world of the text becomes the real world of that person if they can identify their own life in the text.[6] Scholars of hermeneutics, for example Ricoeur, Dilthey, Heidegger and Jeanrond, define the vital purpose of dialogue not only as finding the most probable interpretations, but also as securing self-understanding. Without self-understanding I will not know how to conduct myself in society with some sort of autonomy. In one sense the dialogue can be seen as a dialogue about general interpretations of views of life. At the same time we could say that this dialogue also concerns a personal level and view of life. Personal engagement requires some sort of empathy, mainly in the sense of recognizing the mirror-image of oneself in the face of another person. Empathy means to live out inter-subjectivity, not only to talk about it. Dilthey seems to point this out:

---

[4] Hamrick, 1987, p 30.
[5] Thompson, 1990, p 59.
[6] For Ricoeur's accounts of the world of living speech, the world of the text and its interpretation, cf. Ricoeur, 1990, p 246f., 1991, p 118f., 1992, p 37, Thompson, 1990, pp 47–59.

For everything in which the human spirit has been objectified contains in itself something which is common to the I and the thou. ... Before he learns to speak, the child is already completely immersed in the medium of common contexts. And he learns to understand gestures and facial expressions, motions and exclamations, words and sentences only because they confront him as being always the same, and as always bearing the same relation to that which they signify and express. In this way, the individual becomes oriented in the world of objective spirit.[7]

A Proposal for a Possible Phenomenology

The phenomenology I would support cannot be labelled the 'Phenomenology of Religion', because I do not want to replace what is already known as the Phenomenology of Religion (typological or hermeneutical). My proposal could rather be called a 'Phenomenology within Religious Studies'. My reason is rather trivial; I find phenomenology able to contribute to several other fields of the study of religion besides just the History of Religions with which phenomenology is usually associated. My proposed phenomenology would have the following characteristics which will be discussed below:

1. It will provide us with a third option regarding the realism-anti-realism debate.
2. It will provide us with a definition of the notion of phenomenon which would be applicable to most fields of religious studies.
3. It will consist of a general hermeneutics.
4. It will promote communication in general where dialogue will be one central form of communication.

Realism, Anti-Realism or a Third Option?

All fields of religious studies concern in one way or another human belief in reality beyond and independent of human existence, whether monotheism or polytheism is envisaged. Human responses to transcendent divine reality or to the human situation expressed in commonly accepted doctrines, practices and rituals, are the objects of religious studies. These responses can be observed in (a) expressed experiences, (b) informal or formal structures, for example defined institutions, (c) ethical demands and required consequences of the faith, (d) internal relations within traditions or interrelations between different traditions, (e) overall views of life, (f) images of the object of belief, etc.

The general demand is that claims of beliefs should be justifiable. If religious beliefs are made from the perspective or position of metaphysical realism, we fail to meet that demand since the truth of a religious statement is about a transcendent divine reality existing independent of us.

The position expressed by van der Leeuw, is that we have no access to this independent reality apart from our own expression of our experiences, even though these may be shared by many people. I would say further that in one sense this seems to be the very idea of religion. Yet, we want to say something about

[7] Dilthey, 1977, p 126f.

126

God, and the problem is how to do that and still respect the demand of justification (as discussed in the previous chapter).

The position of metaphysical anti-realism is problematic in relation to beliefs founded on religious faith, since it would either deny the existence of some from us independently existing reality or at least consider it pointless to discuss either the existence or non-existence of such a from us independently existing reality. At the same time, anti-realism seems to be appropriate in relation to phenomenology's epistemic claims that the expressions of experiences are mind-dependent.

Putnam has proposed a third option, i.e., the proposed 'internal realism' which takes into consideration the claims of both positions. In order to find a possible position, which considers both some sort of mind-independent reality and the mind-dependence of language, I support his proposal. Even though Putnam has recently moved away from the position of internal realism, I find it useful for my discussions here. My application of 'internal realism' would be this: the internal aspect is the mind-dependent knowledge and language, since knowledge and experiences are expressed through language. At the same time, we must be aware of our context-dependence, i.e., of the sort of ethnocentrism that Rorty points at. A specific cultural ethnos is expressed within a plurality of cultures and contexts. As I see it, Putnam's term 'world' stands for this contextual pluralism, and it is against that background that we find the realist opening in Putnam's internal realism. The realist aspect consists of a relative mind-independence, conceived as independence in relation to a specific context, i.e., in relation to the particular language which governs the descriptional scheme within the specific context. The demand for justification as Putnam puts it, is not necessarily a demand for a justification here and now, but a demand for a possible justification of our claims, at least in the sense that being based on people's opportunities or shortcomings, it should be able to identify the conditions on which our beliefs could be justified. Thus, this realism is not metaphysical realism, but intra-worldly realism.

Now, this position cannot verify the existence of a metaphysical reality but it allows us to use images of an independent reality. It will also open for us the opportunity to exchange and modify our perspectives through inter-contextual dialogue. Therefore, the phenomenology that I support ascribes itself to the position of internal realism, where the intra-worldly realism is understood in terms of inter-contextuality.

How to Understand the Notion of Phenomenon

This position of internal realism will have consequences for the definition of a phenomenon. I favour van der Leeuw's idea of a phenomenon, which I clarified by means of Husserl's distinction between appearance and the appearing thing, i.e., the remaining conscious content. This corresponds to the distinction between experience as act and the expression of the experience, i.e., of the experienced.

The phenomena of a 'Phenomenology within Religious Studies' would, generally speaking, be the expressions of religious experiences, which in one way or another refer to the encounter with what we seem to understand as a reality independent of us. Instead of making typologies of particulars, of ideal types like prayer, sacrifice, etc., they could be made where tokens refer to views of life, ethical norms, anthropology, world-views, etc. This would allow us to constitute typologies as dimensions. As proposed by Ninian Smart, various apects and functions of religion can be characterized as dimensions of: (1) ritual and praxis, (2) the experiential and emotional, (3) the narrative or mystical, (4) doctrines and philosophy, (5) the ethical and juridical, (6) the social and institutional, and (7) the material objects being used in religious praxis.[8] These dimensions could correspond to the division into subjects, i.e., into scholarly disciplines within fields of religious studies. Each of these dimensions accounts for religious experiences, which are regarded as expressions of religion.

Phenomenology as Hermeneutics

All disciplines contain elements of interpretation. The data would be insignificant unless they are viewed and analyzed against specific perspectives of human life. When perspectives of religious views of life are applied, they are expressed in terms of the aspects described above. The perspectives are not the same for each scholarly subject and therefore I am convinced that no particular discipline can account completely for religion from within its own perspective only. Some exchange of perspectives must therefore take place, so that perspectives can be modified and self-criticism promoted.

Phenomenology, Religious Studies, and Dialogue

The hermeneutical character of my proposed phenomenology also necessitates dialogue. Compared to the discussion on inter-contextuality above, dialogue can be seen as twofold. First, there must be dialogue between the different fields within Religious Studies. Each field would contribute its views and insights according to its schemes of description. This form of interdisciplinary dialogue would create openings for a modification of schemes and perspectives as new ideas and other kinds of knowledge are presented in such a way that new understanding is brought about. In this sense dialogue is, in my opinion, a prerequisite if we want to understand religion in a wider perspective and not only remain within the limited fields that each scholarly discipline represents. Secondly, dialogue is necessary in a broader context as dialogues between different cultural and religious traditions, between religious traditions and the sciences, and also between different sciences. This second level expands the context of discussion by contributing to perspectives from sometimes completely different points of departure, and to some degree from conflicting explanatory models.

Thus, dialogue is not just simply talking to other people. Being able to determine that one particular interpretation of the meanings, motivations, functions, etc. of a particular religious expression is more reasonable than another one, re-

---

[8] Regarding the specifics of each dimension, see Smart, 1989, p 13ff.

128

quires knowledge of one's own tradition, as well as of oneself as a person. This does not contradict the application of epochē and empathy, but rather supports it. Without well-founded insights of oneself and of one's own tradition, epochē would be hard to observe, because one would not know what to refrain from. On this point I find a serious weakness in Rorty's use of too wide a concept of culture. Although moving beyond Rorty's intentions we may still ask ourselves whether anybody can grasp precisely, for example that which is called Western culture, so that their personal identity and the supposed Western identity are made one and the same? Similar arguments can be made in relation to empathy. Without a well-founded awareness of oneself, empathy, i.e., respect and sympathy towards others, is impossible.

It is possible to distinguish between two different levels, where dialogue promotes understanding founded on the interdependency of more than one perspective. In the academic world it is about interdependence between different disciplines and different sciences. At the human level, it is about intersubjectivity.

The hermeneutical phenomenology which I am advocating considers understanding both as self-understanding and as understanding of the other person. It is contextual. It promotes understanding through otherness, which can be both an individual and a collective one. By observing the attitude of presuppositionlessness and the method of bracketing (as described above), it promotes self-distance and helps us to back off from our needs of having the last word. In that way it puts a limit to egocentrism. But this understanding does not imply self-denial as would be the case if I had to copy the life of another person in order to understand the other as well as gaining a perspective on myself.

To understand other people's insights into ways of coping with reality is only possible by means of communication. However, we must not forget that when we talk about what is considered as knowledge gained through religious experiences, the expressions of religious phenomena cannot be regarded as giving a full account of the content of the experience. What is gained is an understanding of other people's or groups of people's own account of what was experienced, which is always interpreted in relation to the context, in which this person or group lives. It is equally important to recognize the integrity of the other as well as of oneself, which I fear can be lost if we really mean that we can leave our own world and cross over and take the place of the other. The point of intersubjectivity is in my opinion the same as the one of Merleau-Ponty, that there should be room both for subjectivity and objectivity, respect for both privacy and individual rights and room for social relations and collective rights.

Coming to the end, how can we claim, against the background of this analysis, that the phenomenology proposed here could provide us with better means to justify religious beliefs?

During this century people have been brought closer to each other, both as a result of societies growing multi-cultural and improved means of communication. All around us we meet people with sometimes very different world-views. In one way or another we have to face the challenges of living with people from other cultures and with other religious creeds.

I have considered the different world-views and views of life as different descriptive schemes. In cases of religious beliefs, each of these descriptive schemes includes the reference to transcendent realities existing independent of us. As long as we live within a specific culture, governed by a particular descriptive scheme, questions of meaning and meaningfulness can be answered without any other challenges than those raised within the system itself. The problem that we are concerned with here occurs above all when we are confronted with several different and sometimes incompatible descriptive schemes within the same society. The fact that all religious beliefs from the various traditions cannot be justified at the same time, because they might contradict each other, causes the question whether it is possible to approach the question of justification differently.

My proposal is that we have to approach a multi-cultural situation through dialogue. The attitude governing these dialogues should be presuppositionlessness towards the others and the bracketing of one's own descriptive scheme/s, which could facilitate coexistence and acceptance of different views of life. This could be the case if we regard the different descriptive schemes as our own products, that is as mind-dependent and not god-given. When regarded as mind-dependent, they become open to questioning and change. This does not stop us from talking about God, but it demands from us the awareness of the fact that we are the ones who are talking. As I see it, it is then possible to combine metaphysical realism—that is belief in transcendent realities existing independent of us—with an epistemological anti-realism—that is with the observance of the fact that we are creating mind-dependent theories also about metaphysical realities, which allow us to talk about God.

Thus we can put our religious beliefs to the test in dialogue with others. Even if it is not necessary with successful justification here and now, we must keep in mind that justification of our claims is required, however we may imagine it. Therefore we must first of all find out how to co-exist with people of other faiths in such a way that there is room for all of us, and so that we can all accept our diversities as options to justification, rather than seeing them as an obstacle for the development and reformation of our different world-views and views of life.

Bibliography

Bach, K.
1995   *Type-token distinction*. In The Cambridge Dictionary of Philosophy. pp 818–819. New York: Cambridge University Press

Barbosa da Silva, A.
1982   *The Phenomenology of Religion as a Philosophical Problem*. Lund: CWK Gleerup

Bleeker, C.J.
1963   *The Sacred Bridge*. Studies in the History of Religions, VII. Leiden: E.J. Brill
1971   *Comparing the religio-historical and the theological method*. In "Numen" 1971 vol. XVIII. pp 9–29 Leiden: E.J. Brill

Brandon, R.
1993   *Heidegger's Categories in "Being and Time"*. In Dreyfus and Hall eds. *Heidegger: A Critical Reader*. pp 45–64 [1992] Oxford UK: Basil Blackwell Ltd

Brenneman, W.L. and Yarian, S.O. and Olson, A.M.
1992   *The Seeing Eye. Hermeneutical Phenomenology in the Study of Religion*. The Pennsylvania State University Press.

Cairns, D.
1973   *Guide for Translating Husserl* The Hague: Martinus Nijhoff

Carman, J.B.
1965   *The Theology of a Phenomenologist*. In "Harvard Divinity Bulletin", 29:3, 1965. pp 13–42

Carr, D.
1991   *Time, Narrative and History*. [1986] Bloomington: Indiana University Press

Chantepie de la Saussaye, P.D.
1905   *Lehrbuch der Religionsgeschichte*. Dritte Vollständig neu bearbeitete Auflage. Tübingen: J.C.B. Mohr

Dalferth, I.
1988   *Theology and Philosophy*. Oxford UK: Basil Blackwell LTD

Dilthey, W.
1962   *Pattern & Meaning in History. Thoughts on History and Society*. Edited and introduced by H.P. Rickman [1961] New York: Harper and Brothers
1977   *Descriptive Psychology and Historical Understanding*. Transl. by R.M. Zaner and K.L. Heiges. The Hague: Martinus Nijhoff

Dreyfus, H. L.
1991   *Being-in-the-World. A Commentary on Heidegger's Being and time, Divison 1*. Cambridge. Mass./London, England: The MIT Press

Dreyfus, H.L. and Hall, H. ed.
1993   *Heidegger: A Critical Reader*. [1992] Cambridge. Mass./Oxford UK: Blackwell Publishers

Dummett, M.
1992   *Truth and Other Enigmas*. [1978] London: Duckworth

Fell, J.P.
1993 *The Familiar and the Strange: On the Limits of Praxis in the Early Heidegger.* In Dreyfus and Hall eds *Heidegger: A Critical Reader.* [1992] pp 65–80. Oxford UK: Basil Blackwell Ltd

Føllesdal, Walløe and Elster.
1985 *Argumentasjonsteori, språk og vitenskapsfilosofi.* [1977] Bergen: Universitetsforlaget AS

Gadamer, H-G.
1993 *Truth and Method.* Translation revised by J. Weinsheimer and D. Marshall, second revised edition [1975, 1989 rev.ed.]. London: Sheed and Ward

Haglund, D.
1977 *Perception, Time and the Unity of Mind, Part 1* Göteborg: Filosofiska Institutionen

Hammond, M., Howart, J. and Keat, R.
1991 *Understanding Phenomenology.* Cambridge. Mass.: Basil Blackwell Inc.

Hamrick, W.S.
1987 *An Existential Phenomenology of Law: Maurice Merleau-Ponty.* Dordrecht: Martinus Nijhoff

Heidegger, M.
1972 *Sein und Zeit.* Tübingen: Max Niemeyer Verlag
1981/1 *Varat och tiden. Vol.1.* Transl. by Matz, R. Lund: Doxa Press
1981/2 *Varat och tiden. Vol.2.* Transl. by Matz, R. Lund: Doxa Press
1982 *The Basic Problems of Phenomenology.* Transl. by Hofstadter, A. Bloomington: Indiana University Press
1984 *The Metaphysical Foundations of Logic.* Transl. by Heim, M. Bloomington: Indiana University Press
1985 *History of the Concept of Time. Prolegomena.* Transl. by Theodore Kisiel. Bloomington and Indianapolis: Indiana University Press
1988 *Hegel's Phenomenology of Spirit.* Transl. by Emand, P. and Maly, K. Bloomington/ Indianapolis: Indiana University Press
1989 *What is Philosophy.* Transl. by W. Kulback and J.T. Wilde. [1963] Plymouth: Vision Press Limited
1992a *Parmenides.* Transl. by Schuwer, A. and Rojcewicz. Bloomington/Indianapolis: Indiana University Press
1992b *The Concept of Time.* Transl. by McNeill, W. [1992] Oxford, UK: Blackwell Publishers
1993a *Heraclitus Seminar.* Together with Eugene Fink. Transl. by Seibert, C.H. [1979] Evanston: Northwestern University Press
1993b *Being and Time.* Translated by J. Macquarrie & E. Robinson. [1962] [1967, 1973, 1978, 1980, 1983, 1985, 1987, 1988, 1990, 1992] Oxford,UK: Blackwell Publishers
1993c *Basic Concepts.* Translated by Cary E. Aylesworth. Bloomington and Indianapolis: Indiana Univeristy Press

Herrmann, E.
1995a *Myt eller verklighet.* In "Om Tolkning IV. Myt-historia-verklighet", Tro & Tanke 1995:3. pp 83–100. Uppsala: Church of Sweden Research Department
1995b *Scientific Theory and Religious Belief. An essay on the rationality of views of life.* Klampen: Kok Pharos Publishing House
1996 *Meaning and Truth in Religion.* Utrechtse Theologische Reeks vol 32. Utrecht: University of Utrecht

Hopkins, B. C.

1993 *Intentionality in Husserl and Heidegger. The Problem of the Original Method and Phenomenon of Phenomenology.* Dordrecht/Boston/London: Kluwer Academic Publishers

Hubbeling, H.G.

1987 *Principles of the Philosophy of Religion.* Assen/Maastricht: Van Gorcum

Hultkrantz, Å.

1973 *Metodvägar inom den jämförande religionsforskningen.* Stockholm: Esselte Studium

Husserl, E.

1928 *Ideen zu einer reinen Phänomenologie und phänomenologische Philosphie 1. Erstes Buch, Allgemeine Einführung in die reine Phänomenologie.* 3 unveränderter Abdruck. Halle a.d.S.: Max Niemeyer Verlag

1965 *Phenomenology and the Crisis of Philosophy.* Transl. by Lauer, Q. New York, Evanston, London: Harper & Row, Publishers

1970a *Philosophie der Arithmetik. Mit ergränzenden textent 1890–1901.* Hrsg. Eley, L. The Hague: Martinus Nijhoff. Husserliana XII

1970b *Logical Investigations.* Transl. by Findlay, J.N. 2 volumes London: Routledge and Kegan Paul

1970c *The Idea of Phenomenology.* Transl. by Alston, W.P. and Nakhnikian, G. 4 impression The Hague: Martinus Nijhoff

1973 *Experience and Judgment. Investigations in a Geneaology of Logic.* Transl. by Churchill, J. S. and Ameriks, K. London: Routledge and Kegan Paul

1975 *Introduction to the Logical Investigations.* Transl. by Bosset, P.J. and Peters, C.H. The Hague: Martinus Nijhoff

1984/1 *Logische Untersuchungen. Zweiter Band, Erster Teil. Untersuchungen zur Phänomenologie und Theorie der Erkenntnis.* Hrsg. Panzer, U. Text der 1. und der 2. Auflage ergränzt durch Annotationen und Beiblätter aus dem Handexemplar. The Hague: Martinus Nijhoff. Husserliana XIX/1

1984/2 *Logische Untersuschungen. Zweiter Band, Zweiter Teil.* Hrsg. Panzer, U, The Hague: Martinus Nijhoff. Husserliana XIX/2

1988 *Cartesian Meditations. An Introduction to Phenomenology.* Transl. by Cairns, D. [1960] 7 impression. Dordrecht: Martinus Nijhoff Publishers

1989 *Fenomenologins idé.* Transl. by Bengstsson, J. Göteborg: Daidalos

1992 *The Phenomenology of Internal Time-Consciousness.* [1964] Indiana University Press / University Microfilms International [1992]

James, G. A.

1985 *Phenomenology and the Study of Religion: The Archaeology of an Approach.* In "The Journal of Religion" 3/1985/vol 65. pp 311–335. Chicago: Chicago University Press

Jaspers, K.

1969 *Philosophy. Volume 1.* Translated by E.B. Ashton. Chicago: Chicago University Press

1970 *Philosophy. Volume 2.* Translated by E.B. Ashton Chicago: Chicago University Press

Jeanrond, W.

1993 *Theological Hermeneutics. Development and Significance.* [1991] London: MacMillan Press LTD

Kluback, W. and Weinbaum, M.

1957 *Dilthey's Philosophy of Existence: Introduction to Weltanschauungslehre.* Translation of an Essay With Introduction. New York: Bookman Associates

Kockelmans, J.J.
1984   *On the Truth of Being. Reflections on Heidegger's Later Philosophy.* Bloomington: Indiana University Press
1994   *Edmund Husserl's Phenomenology.* West Lafayaette: Purdue University Press

Kohák, E.
1978   *Idea and Experience. Edmund Husserl's Project of Phenomenology in Ideas I.* Chicago: The University of Chicago Press

Kolakowski, L.
1987   *Husserl and the Search for Certitude.* Chicago: The University of Chicago Press

Kosso, P.
1992   *Reading the Book of Nature. An introduction to the philosphy of science.* New York: Cambridge University Press

Levin, D.M.
1981   *Reason and Evidence in Husserl's Phenomenology.* [1970] Evanston: Northwestern University Press

Levinas, E.
1985   *The Theory of Intuition in Husserl's Phenomenology.* [1973] Evanston: Northwestern University Press

Lübcke, P. (Ed)
1987   *Vår tids filosofi.* Stockholm: Bokförlaget Forum AB

Makkreel, R.A.
1992   *Dilthey. Philosopher of the Human Studies.* [1975] Princeton: Princeton University Press

Merleau-Ponty, M.
1981   *Phenomenology of Perception.* Transl. by C. Smith. [1961, repr. 1965, 1966, 1967, 1970, 1974, 1976, 1978, 1981] London and Henley: Routledge & Kegan Paul

Okrent, M.
1988   *Heidegger's Pragmatism. Understanding, Being, and the Critique of Metaphysics.* Ithaca and London: Cornell University Press

Palmer, R.E.
1988   *Hermeneutics. Interpretation Theory in Schleiermacher, Dilthey, Heidegger, and Gadamer.* [1969] Evanston: Northwestern University Press

Patočka, J.
1992   *Introduction à la Phénoménologie de Husserl.* Transl. by Erika Abrams. Grenoble: Edition Jerome Million

Pivčević, E.
1970   *Husserl and Phenomenology.* London: Hutchinson and Co LTD

Plantinga, J.R.
1990   *Seeking the Boundaries: Gerardus van der Leeuw on the Study of Religion and the Nature of Theology.* Ontario: McMaster University, J.R. Plantinga

Putnam, H.
1990   *Reason, Truth and History.* [1981, repr. 1982, 1985, 1986, 1987, 1989, 1990] Cambridge US: Cambridge University Press
1992   *Representation and Reality.* [1988, 1991] Cambridge Mass: The MIT Press

Rapaport, H.
1991   *Heidegger & Derrida. Reflections on Time and Language.* [1989] Lincoln and London: University of Nebraska Press

Richir, M.
1987   *Phénomènes Temps et Etres. Ontologie et Phénoménologie.* Edition Jerome Million

Ricoeur, P.
1990   *Time and Narrative, vol. 3.* [1988] Transl. by Blamey, K. and Pellauer, D. Chicago and London: The University of Chicago Press
1991   *From Text to Action. Essays in Hermeneutics, II.* Transl. by Blamey K. and Thompson, J.B. London: The Athlone Press
1992   *Hermeneutics & the Human Sciences.* [1981, 1982 (twice), 1983, 1984, 1985, 1987, 1988, 1989, 1990] Transl. and edited by Thompson, J.B. Paris: Maison des Sciences de l'Homme and Cambridge University Press

Rorty, R.
1993   *Heidegger, Contingency and Pragmatism.* In Dreyfus and Hall eds *Heidegger: A Critical Reader.* pp 209–230 [1992] Oxford UK: Blackwell Ltd
1994   *Objectivity, Relativism, and Truth. Philosophical Papers vol 1.* [1991, repr. 1991, 1993, 1994] Cambridge USA: Cambridge University Press

Ruin, H.
1994   *Enigmatic Origins. Tracing the Theme of Historicity through Heidegger's Works.* Stocholm: Almqvist & Wiksell International

Ryba, T.
1991   *The Essence of Phenomenology and Its Meaning for the Scientific Study of Religion.* Toronto Studies in Religion, Trinity College, University of Toronto, Vol. 7. New York: Peter Lang

Sœlid Gilhus, I.
1984   *The Phenomenology of Religion and Theories of Interpretation.* In "Temenos" vol. 20/1984. pp 26–39. Turku: University of Turku

Sharpe, E. J.
1975   *Comparative Religion. A History.* Bristol: Duckworth

Smart, N.
1989   *The World Religions.* Cambridge: Cambridge University Press

Spiegelberg, H.
1984   *The Phenomenological Movement—a historical introduction.* [1960] [1982] Third revised and enlarged edition. Second impression. The Hague: Martinus Nijhoff

Spinosa, C.
1993   *Derrida and Heidegger: Iterability and Ereignis.* In Dreyfus and Hall eds *Heidegger: A Critical Reader.* [1992] pp 270–297. Oxford UK: Basil Blackwell Ltd

Spranger, E.
1925   *Lebensformen. Geisteswissenschftliche Psychologie und Ethik der Persönlichkeit.* 5 Aufl. Halle: Max Niemeyer

Taminiaux, J.
1991   *Heidegger and the Project of Fundamental Ontology.* Transl. by Gendre, M. Albany: State University of New York Press

Thompson, J.B.
1990   *Critical Hermeneutics. A Study of the Thought of Paul Ricoeur and Jürgen Habermas.* [1981, 1983 (first paperback edition), 1985, 1988] Cambridge, New York, Port Chester, Melbourne, Sydney: Cambridge University Press

Tugendhat, E.
1967   *Der Wahrheitsbegriff bei Husserl und Heidegger.* Berlin: Walter de Gruyter & Co

Valen Sendstad, A.

1969 *Eksistensialfilosofien som fundamentalontologi for åpenbaringsteologien.* Oslo: Universitetsforlagets tryckningssentral.

van der Leeuw, G.

1925 *Einführung in die Phänomenologie der Religion.* München: Verlag von Ernst Reinhardt

1935 *Inleiding tot de Theologie.* Amsterdam: H. J. Paris

1956 *Phänomenologie der Religion.* [1933] Zweite, durchgesehene und erweiterte Auflage, Tübingen: J.C.B. Mohr

1986 *Religion in Essence and Manifestation.* [1938] [1964] New Jersey: Princeton University Press

Waardenburg, J.

1972 *Religion Between Reality and Idea.* in "Numen" Vol XIX, Fasc. 2–3, 1972. Leiden: E.J. Brill

1973 *Classical Approaches to the Study of Religion.* The Hague: Mouton & Co

1978 *Reflections on the Study of Religion.* The Hague: Mouton Publishers

1991a *The Problem of Representing Religions and Religion.* In Klippenberg and Luchesi eds "Religionswissenschaft und Kulturkritik". pp 31–56. Marburg: dialog Verlag

1991b *Scholarship and Subversion: A Response to Donald Wiebe.* In Klippenberg and Luchesi eds "Religionswissenschaft und Kulturkritik". pp 87–92. Marburg: dialog Verlag

Ward, G.

1995 *Barth, Derrida and the Language of Theology.* Cambridge UK: Cambridge University Press